RVP

7

2 7 OCT 2021

ANDY LLOYD-WILLIAMS

RVP

THE BIOGRAPHY OF ROBIN VAN PERSIE

Published by John Blake Publishing Ltd,
3 Bramber Court, 2 Bramber Road,
LondonW14 9PB, England

www.johnblakepublishing.co.uk

www.facebook.com/Johnblakepub facebook
twitter.com/johnblakepub twitter

First published in hardback in 2011
This edition published in 2013

ISBN: 978-1-78219-445-3

British Library Cataloguing-in-Publication Data:

A catalogue record for this book is available from the British Library.

Design by www.envydesign.co.uk

Printed in Great Britain by CPI Group (UK) Ltd

1 3 5 7 9 10 8 6 4 2

Papers used by John Blake Publishing are natural, recyclable products made
from wood grown in sustainable forests. The manufacturing processes conform
to the environmental regulations of the country of origin.

Every attempt has been made to contact the relevant copyright-holders,
but some were unobtainable. We would be grateful if the appropriate
people could contact us.

CONTENTS

PREFACE

Controversy has always lurked just around the corner at every stage of Robin van Persie's life. Tough formative years roaming the back streets of Rotterdam were followed by success and failure in equal measure at some of Europe's best football clubs: van Persie has had ups and downs both on the pitch and behind the scenes. From car crashes and clashes with managers, to netting spectacular, important goals and raising two children, his life has been on a rollercoaster ride of thrills and spills.

It was clear from a young age that van Persie possessed a unique talent. Legend has it that a clairvoyant forecast his rise to success in a chance encounter at an art gallery when he was a child. But whether it be height, dedication or confidence, precocious talent is often accompanied by a limiting factor that the player has to overcome in order to fulfil his potential. This young man struggled with his attitude, as along with that special ability came over-confidence, a fiery tongue and a hot head that made him an unpredictable character on the pitch.

All superheroes have their troubles and weaknesses; the way that they manage to overcome them is part of what makes them super, and van Persie is no different. Superman can't deal with Kryptonite and Spiderman is too compassionate; van Persie has a bit of a temper on him, can be stubborn and has had one or two problems in his personal life.

Many modern footballers have their dark sides. The millions of pounds that 21st-century players command affords them the freedom to do pretty much whatever they like. There are a few lines their money should not allow them to cross but some feel the need to push those boundaries, resulting in broken hearts and brushes with the law.

From Chelsea and England captain John Terry cheating on his wife with ex-teammate Wayne Bridge's girlfriend, to Tottenham striker Jermain Defoe's multiple court appearances over driving offences, many 'big name' players have hit the headlines for the wrong reasons. Van Persie too would run into troubles of his own along a rocky road which included encounters with the police and an incident which would forever taint him in the eyes of many.

But Sir Alex Ferguson, who managed Manchester United to 13 Premier League titles and two Champions League trophies, hailed van Persie as an 'unbelievable' player. Arsène Wenger, the first Premier League manager to assemble a truly global team, called him a 'special talent'.

When he wasn't earning praise from the England top flight's most respected bosses, van Persie also found time to represent his country at three major tournaments, but the Netherlands camp too was never far from controversy. For a man who also has the unfortunate knack of picking up injury after injury, he has had to show real grit and determination to succeed.

CHAPTER 1

EARLY DAYS

Robin van Persie was born in the Kralingen district of eastern Rotterdam on 6 August 1983. His father Bob raised Robin and sisters Lilly and Kiki as a single parent after splitting from their mother when Robin was five years old. Both Bob and Robin's mother José Ras were artists – a strong link to his creativity on the football field. Pushy parents have a reputation of ruining children's football matches so perhaps coming from a less football-intense home allowed Robin to concentrate on developing his skills without the extra pressure some football-mad parents can put on their offspring.

He told Arsenal TV that it was a very different household to those of his friends as he was granted a bit more freedom than the average kid. Arranging sleepovers for pals was a lot easier for van Persie to do because his parents were so relaxed. He said: 'We were free! The weekend is for yourself – enjoy yourself!'

His parents attempted to persuade van Persie to follow in their steps as an artist, but he always found football much more of a draw than painting and sculpting. Bob was a famous artist in the Dutch cultural scene but despite some early forays into the world of art, the lure of a football always proved too strong for van Persie to resist. After his parents divorced, Robin lived with Bob in an artistic den and was continually encouraged to be creative. He told the *Independent*: 'When I was younger my parents encouraged me to be creative, to draw and play games to expand my mind. They wanted me to be an individual. But it turned out I'm rubbish with my hands.'

In fact it was van Persie's grandfather, who had himself played football professionally, who encouraged him in those early years. The pair used to play for hours on an area of grass behind his grandparents' home.

The young lad took to the city streets where he would play football for up to eight hours a day with other youngsters. He did a lot of growing up in the concrete jungle as it showed what the real world was like: for better and for worse. In his early teens young Robin didn't have a lot of money but playing was free so long as somebody had brought a ball.

He would go on to marry a Dutch-Moroccan girl and it was his time on the streets that introduced van Persie to Moroccan and Surinamese communities. An upbringing encompassing different communities would make him a well-balanced, worldly adult. He may not have become the artist his parents wanted but the fact he was raised in an artistic environment is clear for all to see. Van Persie has always had a very distinctive style on the pitch, clearly thinking outside of the box and, in his early days at least, possessing something of a temper.

SBV Excelsior saw great potential in van Persie and the local club played a great part in his early development. The Rotterdam outfit acted as a 'satellite club' for its more illustrious neighbours Feyenoord, providing stars of the future for the big boys up the road. They identified and nurtured a host of future Premier League stars including Winston Bogarde, George Boateng and Salomon Kalou.

Roughly translated from Latin, 'Excelsior' means 'onward and upward' and it was certainly the case for van Persie after he learned his trade there. Excelsior's ground holds a tiny 3,531 people and the club is known for providing a relaxed environment in which players can properly focus on development and hone their skills. Joining the youth set-up at his hometown club at the age of four, van Persie grew up playing for the club and did not leave until he was 16.

Truth be told he had probably already outgrown Excelsior and it would have been time to move on anyway, but the reason van Persie left for Feyenoord was a series of disagreements with coaching staff.

His fiery temper regularly attracted trouble at school: in his early teenage years Robin was in hot water pretty much every day. He was sent out of the classroom so regularly that a friendship was struck up with the school janitor, who coincidentally was Dutch-Moroccan. School caretaker Sietje Moush became a valuable friend who could be trusted for advice.

Van Persie told the *Independent*: 'If you're 15, 16, 17, it's a difficult age. You start wanting to go out, to clubs or whatever, but my friend made sure I never did. He'd say, "Those places are rubbish", and I believed it. When I was sent out it was never because I yelled at the teacher or used bad words. I was more the wise guy, taking the piss. I always had something to say back to the teacher, which I'm sure was frustrating for them, but I always had respect.' Such was the respect between the pair that Moush would go on to act as van Persie's unofficial agent.

That wise guy-based trouble spilled over onto the football field. Coaches were not willing to put up with what was at times a petulant attitude and van Persie moved on to satellite club Feyenoord, where he would make his debut at just 17.

Those old wounds have since been forgotten; everybody says things they don't really mean when they're young. The club have been keen to maintain contact with van Persie in subsequent years, so in October 2010 he was appointed as an ambassador of the club and one of the Stadion Woudestein stands was named after him.

He may have only been 27 at the time but van Persie told Dutch reporters he was already hatching plans to return to the club at the end of his career. It looked as though van Persie meant what he said when he attended a celebratory evening at Stadion Woudestein. Most footballers simply 'turn up' at events like this, look slightly awkward, smirk, perform whatever duties are demanded of them and make a sharp exit. Robin van Persie is not most footballers. Not only did he avoid making that sharp exit, he also led a conga line in the supporters' bar and belted out an endearingly tuneless version of 'You'll Never Walk Alone' in a karaoke session. Not many big-name footballers would be willing to get this hands-on with supporters but van Persie didn't seem to have a problem with it. Quite the opposite in fact: it looked like he was thoroughly enjoying himself.

Dutch radio reporters managed to grab van Persie in a brief quiet moment and he said: 'It may only be a small ground but I do not know when, whether I'm 33 or 38 I do not know, but I would like to return as a player at Excelsior. I started here so I feel it would complete the circle for me. Many people forget that for me it all started with Excelsior. I had already been playing football for some time before I could be seen on TV playing for Feyenoord. From the age of five onwards I was to be found almost daily at Excelsior. That time was great.'

As with every moment in van Persie's career, disaster was only just around the corner. But surely nothing could go wrong at a stand renaming ceremony? The injury curse that plagued various stages of his career struck again but this time it was an unfortunate child who was in the firing line. As he led a line of kids along the side of the pitch, a camera crew was in hot pursuit.

Curiosity got the better of one of the youngsters and he looked back towards the camera and not the direction he was walking in. As he turned to look the way he was walking, the unfortunate child walked straight into a pole and fell to the ground in tears. Van Persie looked concerned and did his best to console the bawling child after helping him to his feet.

After falling out with coaches at Excelsior he made a fresh start at Feyenoord. The club was still in his home of Rotterdam but was one of the 'big three' of Dutch football –

Feyenoord, PSV and Ajax battled for supremacy in the Eredivisie.

A spate of injuries in the Feyenoord squad afforded van Persie a chance sooner than he might have hoped and he made his debut in the 2001/2002 season at just 17 years of age. It was 'sink or swim' as he was thrown in at the deep end but some young players can enter the highest level playing with no fear and that can provide a breath of fresh air for all concerned. This was the case for van Persie as he shot to prominence in a season that culminated in winning the KNVB Best Young Talent award.

That early rise to prominence might, in a roundabout kind of way, have been to his detriment, a victim of his own success. Coach Bert van Marwijk thought he needed to be brought back down to earth and, as at Excelsior, van Persie fell out with the boss. Feyenoord is the wrong club to play for if you are a tad arrogant. The 'Sleeping Giants', or 'Slapende Reus' in Dutch, think arrogance belongs at their Amsterdam rivals Ajax and look to snuff out any trace of it from their players.

In the youth set-up he played alongside Civard Sprockel, who would go on to join Vitesse, and Said Boutaha, who has played for a string of Eredivisie clubs. It soon became clear that van Persie was going to be a decent proposition, and by the time he reached 18 the De Kuip club awarded him a three and a half year contract. The long-term deal was part of Feyenoord's policy of nurturing local talent and also meant they would be in a strong bargaining position if he were to attract the attentions of a club with money to spend. Arsenal would eventually come calling but van Persie was still a few years away from his dream move to north London.

As a headstrong young man, van Persie was unable to handle a relentless stream of criticism coming from his coaches. Things were clearly starting to get to him and soon the young hopeful was not only challenging van Marwijk but also back-chatting to his Netherlands Under-21 manager Foppe de Haan and Dutch footballing icon Pierre van Hooijdonk, who starred as the side won the UEFA Cup in 2002.

It would be hard to spot in the moment, but a few years on van Persie said he understood why some people had come to think that he was an over-confident, arrogant player. He told the *Daily Express*: 'I can understand it if people say I am arrogant. Recently I saw myself on TV and I thought, "Well, well, well Robin, you have a nasty swagger." A little less would be better. But that attitude says nothing about my personality, but more about my image. I don't blame anybody who thinks I am arrogant because I think it also myself.'

That image might have been 'part of the package' when he played in Arsenal's galaxy of stars but it was different at Feyenoord. Van Marwijk was a hard coach who liked his players to be modest and quiet working machines that he could easily control, not expressive free-thinkers who were always off doing their own thing.

Pierre van Hooijdonk was the star of the show but young upstart van Persie was extremely confident in his own ability and at times ignored the great. In a game against RKC Waalwijk, van Hooijdonk set himself to take a free-kick but van Persie nipped in and took it first, his effort flying over the crossbar.

Van Persie told the *Independent*: 'The shot did not go in but I was feeling good at the time. I still think he could have been a bit more polite, he could have said "OK take it." Now I can say, "Robin, maybe you should have let that free-kick go." It was a fantastic position for me. The position of the ball was for a left-footed player but he was the free-kick taker and he made a big problem out of it. That's OK. I think it would have been the smart thing to let him take it. For me it was no big problem, those kinds of things happen. I learned from that moment.'

It was incidents like that which would see van Marwijk relegate him to the bench and reserves after initially impressing. It is fair to say the coach did not quite understand or agree with the way van Persie went about his business. After he had joined Arsenal and found himself better understood by Arsène Wenger, van Persie complained that his relationship with van Marwijk had never been quite right and he had been misunderstood.

Indeed it would have been easy to mistake this youthful hunger for arrogance when in fact it was a childhood spent playing street football that had made him this way. When the kids of Kralingen played their intense 'winner stays on' games, if they did not go out of their way to showcase skills, they would very quickly find themselves watching from the sidelines.

Van Persie burst onto the scene at Feyenoord as a raw but exciting centre forward who had an eye for the spectacular, and netted eight goals in his first season. Those disciplinary problems were evident early in his career as he also received a red card early doors. He netted his first goal after coming off the bench in a 4-2 victory over FC Twente and, with the club going through a terrible injury crisis, he was given the chance to start against arch-rivals Ajax. Van Persie really made people sit up and notice as he netted again in the 1-1 draw. That brilliant start to his Feyenoord career continued when he scored in a 4-1 win over AZ Alkmaar.

It was at Rangers that van Persie made his European debut for the Dutch outfit, as the side went on to win the competition. As the sides met in the second leg in the Netherlands, van Persie cut in from the flank and crashed a drive against the post. For an unknown he had played a massive part in getting the side to the UEFA Cup final as he set up Pierre van Hooijdonk to score in the semi-final second leg.

Van Persie started that final and showed flashes of brilliance as his team beat Borussia Dortmund 3-2 to lift the trophy on their own patch. It was a fantastic start to his career to lift the UEFA Cup in front of his own supporters and the young star was understandably over the moon.

It is the understatement of the century to say that van Persie and van Marwijk did not see eye to eye. On the verge of the club's UEFA Super Cup clash against Real Madrid, the coach sent van Persie home from the club's training camp in Turkey, saying he did not like van Persie's body language upon being asked to warm up for a UEFA Champions League qualifying game.

After he joined Arsenal, van Persie looked back at that incident with regret. He told the *Independent*: 'Feyenoord took Real Madrid away from me very, very rudely. Imagine you're 19, you're only a few months as a professional and they do that to you. Real were the best in the world then, the biggest test for a footballer, and it was my dream to play against Zinedine Zidane. He's such an amazing footballer, his first touch, his vision. I have big respect for him, more than for David Beckham.'

Looking back on his frustrating time at De Kuip, van Persie said: 'That's just not the way – belittling people is just not enjoyable. That is not the way to help a talented youngster on his way.'

A more mature van Persie is able to reflect on his Feyenoord years and learn from them rather than just vent his frustrations. He said that the club's coaches had set bad examples to their up and coming young players. He was not the only one to have coaches constantly niggling away at him, but while players with a more formal football upbringing were used to being treated like this, van Persie simply could not accept being spoken to in such a manner. Rather than put up and shut up as might have been wiser for him to do, van Persie answered back to van Marwijk in the same way he had done to his teachers at school.

When he was at Arsenal, van Persie was able to admit that he had created his own problems at Feyenoord: 'I don't want to make excuses for myself because I did make some real mistakes. But that was mainly because of the emotions, because I did not have the self-control and could not control the situation.'

That restraint would come in time and eventually van Persie stopped lashing out so much in high-pressure situations.

Van Persie said it was poor communication that led him to fall out with van Marwijk. Perhaps he had been naive to think he could stroll up to the manager and make suggestions about how to conduct training sessions: 'There were a few misunderstandings with the coach, a few miscommunications. Sometimes I went to him to have a talk but I think he thought I was trying to tell him what to do. I went with good intentions – to say what I thought about the team and my position in it.'

Arsène Wenger would later convert him from a winger to a striker but van Marwijk was not so keen to mix things up. After van Persie had suggested he might do well in a more central role, van Marwijk told reporters he had been demanding a place in the side: 'He said in the papers afterwards that I was demanding to be in the team as a second striker. It wasn't like that. I just suggested that he try me in another position some time to see how it worked out. I was unhappy on the left wing, so why stay quiet?'

Badmouthing his player to the press would not help anybody. When Wenger had problems with a player he would try to spur them on with a quiet word in the ear rather than having a go at them in public. Wenger would later show van Marwijk how things were done when he listened to his player's suggestions instead of moaning to reporters.

This harsh treatment seemed to be the way things worked in Rotterdam. Van Persie told the *Independent* that after constant criticism from van Marwijk, the press had played its part in his descent into notoriety at De Kuip. Once his manager had turned on him and banished the young star to the reserves, the media tried every trick in the book to blacken his name, including hounding his father. After van Persie returned to the first team and hit a fine vein of form, the fickle reporters were soon waxing lyrical about the striker and, looking back on that period, he said it toughened him up and taught him to ignore what was written.

He said: 'They took my dad and painted him very black. I was 19, I'd just come into the real world, and it was hard.

Then a few months later, when I had a good period again, I thought, "These people who absolutely hammered me are writing great things about me again", and since then I haven't cared what they say.'

After breaking into the Feyenoord first team as an 18-year-old, van Persie quickly fell on hard times after squabbling with his manager and was, on reflection, lucky to escape the nightmare and seek a fresh start at Arsenal. Furthermore, there was a lot of bad blood between Feyenoord, Ajax and PSV Eindhoven and somehow van Persie had managed to get himself caught up in it. He was usually not exactly the shy and retiring type but the marriage of Robin and Bouchra Elbali was held in secret in April 2004 for fear of the ceremony attracting the wrong kind of attention.

It later emerged that in a low-key ceremony, only van Persie's parents, his sister and Bouchra's family had been present. The *Mail on Sunday* said the wedding took place because Bouchra was a Muslim and would not have been able to live with her long-term partner if they were not married. Robin was not a Muslim but wanted to help Bouchra respect her religion's traditions and codes of conduct.

CHAPTER 2

THE DREAM MOVE

It sounds like a classic case of fabricated football club propaganda but van Persie, a lad raised in a working class area of Rotterdam, claims he grew up supporting Arsenal. He admired Robert Pires, Thierry Henry and (it goes without saying) a certain goalscoring machine going by the name of Dennis Bergkamp.

Van Persie was, somewhat predictably, introduced to English supporters as 'the new Bergkamp'. The comparisons were obvious – Dutch, attacking, delicate players with good looks to boot. In his youth van Persie would have had Dennis Bergkamp rammed down his throat as he was such a successful, popular player – the inspiration behind many wins for both club and country. Bergkamp would go on to be voted the second best player in the history of Arsenal by the club's fans and certainly gave van Persie something to aspire to.

Van Persie did not feel the need to hide the love he felt for his fellow countryman, telling the *Times*: 'For many years Bergkamp was the star player I absolutely adored. I must have studied every one of his tricks with the ball.'

Bergkamp was from a different generation of Dutch players to van Persie but the two still had the chance to play together as Bergkamp stayed at the club until 2006, despite many fans assuming van Persie had been drafted in as his replacement.

Robin van Persie signed for Arsenal on 17 May 2004 for the modest fee of £2.75 million, with wages reportedly set at £25,000 a week. At the time not a lot was known about the 20-year-old who was only a Netherlands Under-21 international at that stage. That did not detract from how much of a bargain his transfer fee was – the same summer Wayne Rooney had cost Manchester United nearly 10 times as much with a deal worth over £25 million.

It was a dream move for van Persie but at the same time he had a hard task ahead. He told the *Evening Standard*: 'It's been a huge challenge for me. In Arsenal's terms I wasn't a big money signing. So I knew that when a chance came, even if it was only for two or three minutes, I would have to make the most of it. Every minute, every training session I try to improve.'

He had been courted by the club for quite some time beforehand but it was reported that Feyenoord wanted to hold out for something closer to the £5 million mark. After five long months of negotiations, Arsenal had their man.

Chief scout Steve Rowley was the driving force behind the deal and he was the man who travelled many times to watch van Persie in action. After van Persie spectacularly fell out with van Marwijk – during one bust-up allegedly hurling his boots across the dressing room – van Persie was banished to the reserves in the spring of 2004. This was a move that could have spelled the end of Arsenal's interest and potentially wrecked van Persie's career. Amazingly, and thankfully for van Persie, Rowley was not deterred by this and travelled to watch van Persie turn out for Feyenoord's reserve side against bitter rivals Ajax.

The average reserve game is played at a snail's pace and attended by one man and his dog – if the dog can be bothered to turn up – but when Feyenoord and Ajax are playing, it is anything but an average game. When the rivals' second strings met on 15 April 2004, it's fair to say all hell broke loose. Four thousand hostile Ajax supporters lined the perimeter of the pitch and van Persie was drenched with beer every time he went near the touchline. Rowley must have been impressed when van Persie responded to this intimidation by raising his game. The Arsenal-Tottenham rivalry might have been this strong but it certainly wouldn't be this hands-on (or beer-on). At full time some hooligans ran onto the pitch, attacking Jorge Acuña and van Persie, who feared for his life.

Ajax youth coach Marco van Basten sprinted into the resulting melee to rescue the young star, who was in serious trouble. Emerging with severe bruising to his neck and back, he later told the press it was 'no exaggeration' to say he thought he was going to die in the carnage.

Less than two weeks later, the transfer to Arsenal was rubber stamped and van Persie was saved from this nightmare. It seemed everything that could have gone wrong in Rotterdam did, and he must have considered himself very fortunate to have been able to salvage a move to the reigning Premier League champions from the flaming wreckage of his Feyenoord career.

Van Persie was quick to salute the belief Rowley showed in him: 'I know the manager gets all the credit, but I think Steve Rowley is just as important for Arsenal. Every young player at Arsenal gets to know him first. And when I look at the quality of the young players we have, you can only say the club does a fantastic job every season.'

Steve Rowley would continue to play an important role in van Persie's Arsenal career as the pair would regularly sit down to sift through hours of video-taped match action together. The wily scout was not afraid to highlight things van Persie had done wrong in matches because he knew the Dutchman would not take offence and only wanted to learn and grow as a player. Rowley had even been known to chip in with suggestions to help van Persie improve his game.

Arsène Wenger was very pleased with the capture of van Persie, praising his skills and adaptability. Shortly after he signed, a club statement read: 'Robin is a great young talent and a fantastic signing for the club. He has a great left foot and is a great passer with excellent vision. He can play as a striker or on the wing. Robin has shown great potential at both club and under-21 international level and will help to strengthen our squad considerably.'

Van Persie said Wenger took no time at all to win him over and the pair instantly clicked: 'It took Wenger 10 minutes to gain my trust. Wenger told me that I'm a great player but that I need patience. He said to me, "When you go past Campbell or Kolo Touré in training, then you will play in my team."'

That strong bond was an extremely important factor in van Persie making it through an extremely challenging first year at the north London club. Wenger would be there when his young star needed him the most. It was a period of change in the Arsenal front line as £13 million France striker Sylvain Wiltord had fallen out of favour and would not be offered a new contract that summer, along with the aging Nwankwo Kanu, who had lined up a move to West Bromwich Albion after the Arsenal bench had started to give him splinters.

The club's iconic 'Invincibles' squad had just managed to win the Premier League by going an entire season unbeaten but there was no time for sentiment in Wenger's eyes so it was out with the old and in with the new. Dennis Bergkamp was in his mid-thirties and surely only had a few seasons left in the tank, so van Persie was the fresh blood the Gunners desperately needed. With Bergkamp and Thierry Henry – at the time two of the best strikers in the world – both very much in their pomp, it would take van Persie time to get his chance in the side and as he matured the hot-head would have to learn the art of patience as he waited his turn.

Van Persie said it was like a dream come true to sign for a club like Arsenal and he must have been thrilled to link up with household names Bergkamp, Henry and Robert Pires in pre-season training. He had hardly made a good first impression in the dressing room, wearing blue and white clothes when he first met his new Arsenal team mates. Captain Patrick Vieira immediately noticed he was stood there in the colours of arch rivals Tottenham and made a jokey comment. Van Persie had been blissfully unaware of the rivalry with Spurs but his dress had broken the ice and the dressing room banter could commence.

In a typically understated interview with the club website, Bergkamp said van Persie was 'quite a talent' and 'obviously knows what he's doing'. He was never one for going over the top with his words and Bergkamp was probably keen for van Persie to follow his example and let his feet do the talking. At the end of the day, for a footballer what happens during the match is all that matters, and maybe it was time for van Persie to follow the senior player's lead and only pay attention to what was happening on the pitch.

Those feet were chattering away when Robin van Persie scored on his Arsenal debut as the Gunners thrashed neighbours Barnet 10-1 – van Persie netting in the 30th minute against the Conference side. He followed this up with goals in his next two games – a 3-2 win at NK Maribor and a 2-1 victory at Grazer AK.

He had made good ground early on but that fresh start would have to wait a little while as there was to be a Dutch kick in the tail. The 20-year-old had to return to the Netherlands when Arsenal took part in the pre-season Amsterdam Tournament. Van Persie started the opening game on 30 July at the Amsterdam Arena against River Plate in the 'Bergkamp role' – sitting just behind striker Francis Jeffers – as the former Ajax man watched on from the bench. Some clever play with Jeffers and Jermaine Pennant looked promising and van Persie would have been relatively pleased with the way he was playing. The Amsterdam public appeared less than impressed with the man who had previously starred for their bitter rivals and his every touch was booed and jeered. It wasn't quite as ridiculous as being assaulted by Ajax fans following a reserve game but it was still strange to see a crowd behaving like this in a pre-season friendly. A former Tottenham star playing against Arsenal would certainly not have come under such fire during a friendly match.

Things only got worse on the journey back to Arsenal's hotel when van Persie came face to face with members of the public. As van Persie and his wife Bouchra neared the team's Hilton Hotel, two men on bikes approached their car, began shouting abuse and spat at the star through his open window.

Van Persie told the *Evening Standard*: 'Two guys on bikes started yelling at me and spat at me through the open window. They kicked the car three or four times and spat again. They drove after us but could not keep up. It was unbelievable.'

The couple were shocked by the incident and van Persie would surely now be even more eager to make a good impression at Arsenal with bridges seemingly burned in his home country. That defiant characteristic spotted by Arsenal chief scout Steve Rowley was there for van Persie's team mates to see as he came off the bench in the game against Ajax the next day. Despite the heavy barracking he was given, van Persie got on with the game – taking free-kicks and skipping past opponents as if he had ear plugs in and was blissfully unaware of what was going on around him. The fact that at the age of 20 he was able to handle such an atmosphere would have impressed Wenger and surely boded well for future derby fixtures against Spurs.

Ajax manager Ronald Koeman said the barracking given

to van Persie in this second game was shameful. It came just months after that reserve team incident and Koeman told the *Evening Standard*: 'Van Persie is a great talent. After what happened here a couple of months ago he deserved a different reception. That was appalling.'

Van Persie had shown the Ajax fans that he would not be affected and said after the game that he just wanted to move on from the two incidents. He was keen not to tar all Ajax fans with the same brush – probably a wise move when you take into consideration the fact that the Dutch national side use the Amsterdam Arena to host some of their fixtures, so he would be back at some point in the not too distant future. After the game he said: 'What happened in April is history to me. It was done by a few guys who cannot be called real fans. I want to forget about it, and hope things like that will never happen again.'

His Arsenal career was off with a bang as van Persie made his debut in the 3-1 Charity Shield win against Manchester United at the Millennium Stadium in Cardiff in August 2004. While Wembley stadium was being redeveloped, English domestic finals were played in the Welsh capital. José Antonio Reyes ran the show for Arsenal as they hit three in the second half and it was clear van Persie was the new kid on the block. When Reyes had got in behind the United defence and was bearing down on Tim Howard's goal, van Persie was up alongside him just waiting for the ball to be squared. Instead Gilberto powered in front of the new man and gleefully smacked the ball home as van Persie half-heartedly celebrated what could have been his first competitive goal in Arsenal colours had his team mates allowed it to happen.

As Arsenal overawed United, van Persie squandered the opportunity to score a perfect opening goal when his mentor-to-be Dennis Bergkamp crossed from the right. Van Persie did well to beat his man to the ball but his near-post header cannoned into the side-netting. Thierry Henry and Reyes were much sharper than van Persie that day and this would set the tone for the opening months of the season.

It would be a tough transition from the more measured attitude of the Eredivisie to the fast-paced, full-blooded action of the Premier League. His new manager said it was only natural that van Persie would take months to adjust to life in England. The Dutchman had quite a slender build and would certainly receive his fair share of knocks to welcome him to the country.

Wenger said: 'I feel there is an adaptation for a young player coming to English football of six and eight months to adjust to the pace of the game and the physical challenges. I was pleased with the way he used his body against Sunderland, that was his problem when he arrived here because it is not as physical as that in Holland.'

This transitional period took longer than it might have done because Wenger decided that van Persie needed to move in from his favoured position on the wing to find more joy in a central role. Thierry Henry had been transformed in a similar way after being signed as a winger from Italian giants Juventus only to go on to become one of the world's best strikers, and Wenger clearly believed he could replicate this success with van Persie.

Midway through van Persie's second season at the club, when he was scoring for fun from a central position, Wenger said: 'It's quite strange as Robin was educated as a winger and played at Feyenoord only as a winger. I tried at the start to play him as a winger but felt he didn't really have that game, with mobility trying to go behind players. So I put him more central.'

There was another piece of off-the field drama for van Persie in October as he was once again involved in an incident with his car. Not content with being spat and sworn at in Amsterdam, van Persie took his poor vehicle one step further when he smashed it into the central reservation of the M25 motorway before crashing into a field. Foolishly van Persie then phoned a friend to pick him up and left the wreckage of his £65,000 BMW. Police later traced him to Arsenal's Colney training ground where he was questioned.

His 'mentor' Dennis Bergkamp played the role of interpreter and told police van Persie had panicked and had no idea it was an offence to leave the scene of a crash. An Arsenal source told the *Evening Standard*: 'Robin had no idea he was doing wrong by leaving the scene of the crash. He went to a phone box and called a colleague to pick him up. He was very shaken.' He eventually escaped punishment after claiming to have not fully understood the road regulations and saying he had needed his team mate to take him out of a stressful situation to make sure he was on time for that day's training session.

Arsenal had extended the previous season's unbeaten league run to almost the end of that month, but as they looked to make it 50 games without defeat they suffered their own crash as they neared the Manchester United junction of the Premier League motorway. Van Persie was an unused substitute at Old Trafford as the home side ran out 2-0 winners after a hotly disputed Ruud van Nistelrooy penalty and Wayne Rooney's clincher at the death.

But the action really kicked off after the final whistle had been blown when the two sets of players clashed in the tunnel. As they hurled obscenities at each other, a slice of pizza was launched at United manager Sir Alex Ferguson. Ashley Cole described the scene in his biography: 'This slice of pizza came flying over my head and hit Fergie straight in the mush... all mouths gawped to see this pizza slip off this famous face and roll down his nice black suit.'

Van Persie's next start came in the same city a few days later as a youthful team headed to Manchester City in the League Cup – a competition low on Arsène Wenger's list of priorities. The Arsenal players were greeted by a tongue in cheek 'no pizza or soup for safety reasons' notice as they walked into the away dressing room. The competition seems to have been of little importance to Arsenal throughout the club's history as various managers have fielded weakened sides in a competition they have won just two times compared to 10 FA Cup wins and 13 league championships.

Wenger had all the excuses on hand ahead of the game. He said: 'Those who played on Sunday [at Old Trafford] are on the fringe of injury and many of them just at the limit of being able to play. So at the moment I cannot risk any players because we have so many who are just on the fringe of being injured. Robin van Persie is a big talent in the role Dennis Bergkamp plays for us. He can create, he can score and I am confident he will have a good game.'

It was hardly a classic but once again van Persie was able to get on the score sheet as he gave Arsenal the lead in a 2-1 win. After initially fluffing his lines as he completely missed the ball following a generous cut-back from Quincy Owusu-Abeyie, van Persie showed composure to bury a similar chance that fell to him later in the game.

The young guns had shown what they were capable of and Wenger said van Persie's goal was a 'real Arsenal goal' – praise indeed. The emerging Arsenal stars had done themselves proud and Wenger told the *Evening Standard*: 'The next generation looks very good. It makes me convinced the club has a future. The scouts and the coaching staff, they are getting the good young boys in. We have concentrated on that for the last few years and now, slowly, you start to see the quality.'

This would have been a real confidence boost for van Persie and he was on a roll as Southampton cruised into town for a Premier League game the following Saturday. The defeat at Old Trafford was bad enough but to lose at home to the struggling Saints would have been a complete disaster. The Gunners had led through a Thierry Henry strike but a late Rory Delap double looked to have nicked all three points for the south coast club. Wenger said he was worried the side had a hangover from the previous week but in complete contrast to the rest of the team van Persie came into the game with his tail up after that midweek win.

He came on for Freddie Ljungberg with just over five minutes left and in that short window of time managed to cut inside a defender and curl a shot into the top corner to score his first ever Premier League goal and salvage a point for the home side. Van Persie could have won the game in stoppage time with a much easier opportunity but he could only direct his header straight at goalkeeper Antti Niemi.

People kept saying it was the time for van Persie to elbow

his way into contention and it sounds like he listened to them when Arsenal travelled back to Old Trafford for a League Cup match at the start of a busy December. United striker David Bellion's goal after 19 seconds settled the game but all the talk was about van Persie, who stole the headlines for all the wrong reasons.

As the second half began, he was involved with an unsightly clash with Kieran Richardson and swung an elbow the way of his United counterpart. Richardson lashed out in retaliation and it is fair to say all hell broke loose as a result. After the drama of their last few meetings there had hardly been any love lost between Arsenal and United. Although both sides showed the competition their usual respect by fielding teams full of young and fringe players, the clash still had plenty of bite.

Van Persie quickly found himself surrounded by a pack of irate United players as referee Mark Halsey attempted to restore some kind of calm. Yellow cards were dished out to both men as the official tried to calm the situation, and van Persie would have considered himself extremely lucky to still be on the pitch. Richardson sought some revenge at the end of the game when he clattered into his Dutch friend and Halsey immediately blew the full-time whistle to prevent things from getting out of hand.

United boss Sir Alex Ferguson was predictably fuming at the final whistle and demanded that the FA take further action. He said: 'Van Persie was lucky to stay on. The FA must look at it because the boy threw an elbow. I asked the referee why both players had been booked, he said "for aggressive intent" and told me he had not seen the elbow.'

Wenger later admitted it deserved more than a yellow

card and – although he would have been pleased with the fire in van Persie's belly – might have been that little bit more hesitant to put van Persie in his starting line-up. After the game Wenger said his young star had to learn to keep his calm, something he thought van Persie was already capable of after dealing so well with that backlash in Amsterdam just months beforehand. He said: 'Robin shows great potential but he must also learn to keep his nerves under control and not get over-excited. I considered taking him off because he was involved in some heated moments. He must learn to keep calm.'

He may have been limited to these substitute appearances but van Persie was making the most of them and doing his chances of starting more matches no harm at all. When he came on as a second half substitute to score the final goal in Arsenal's 5-1 Champions League humiliation of Rosenborg, his strike made it the Gunners' biggest ever win in the competition at Highbury. With the part-time Norwegian champions run ragged by a rampant Arsenal, van Persie could have hit a hat-trick but after a couple of misses had to be happy with just the one goal. He was smartly set up by Reyes and dinked the ball over the advancing goalkeeper. Wenger joked after the game, 'Maybe we were never as bad as people said we were.'

His game time was seriously limited but as 2004 drew to a close van Persie ruffled a few feathers with a feisty showing as Arsenal stayed within five points of leaders Chelsea with a 1-0 win at Newcastle. Vieira's first half goal settled it after van Persie had hammered several shots at Shay Given – one striking the Irish goalkeeper in the face and another drawing a more conventional sprawling save.

It is fair to say this wasn't a vintage performance. *Telegraph* reporter Henry Winter remarked that the club's younger Dutchman was very much a poor man's Dennis Bergkamp rather than a more youthful version of the club legend. Van Persie would then flash a sight of the dark side to his game after letting wind-up merchant Lee Bowyer get under his skin. Bowyer feigned injury after a tame van Persie tackle to draw a dangerous free-kick for the hosts, before a hot-headed tackle on Steven Taylor which may have only drawn a yellow card but showed that van Persie had not grown out of the petulant attitude that got him into trouble back home in years gone by.

The continued absence of José Antonio Reyes gave the Dutchman a chance to impress as Arsenal travelled to South London neighbours Charlton Athletic on New Year's Day. Charlton kept them at bay in a quiet opening to 2005 that hardly fired a warning shot across the bows of title rivals Chelsea and Manchester United. They eventually awoke from that extended lie-in and it was van Persie who was the catalyst as Arsenal took the lead 10 minutes before the break. He did well to hold up possession before finding captain Patrick Vieira, who fed Freddie Ljungberg to score.

The hosts equalised on the stroke of half-time but Swede Ljungberg doubled his tally straight after the restart after Cesc Fàbregas' clever back-heel. Now it was van Persie's time to shine and he grabbed the chance with both hands when it presented itself. The lead up to his goal must have had supporters in the away end wondering if they had come to watch the right team because it was not the type of goal they usually scored. Young defender Justin Hoyte punted a somewhat uncultured ball up the field and it looked like the unimaginative delivery would be dealt with easily by the Addicks' defence. But when van Persie caught the faintest whiff of a goal-scoring opportunity, he was on to it like a shot and he made the most of Jonathan Fortune's blunder to put Arsenal 3-1 up. The Charlton man miscued a header aimed back towards his goalkeeper and van Persie nipped in to crash a sumptuous left-footed effort straight through the helpless Dean Kiely and just inside the far post. He ran over to celebrate in front of the jubilant Arsenal fans housed behind the goal and it looked like 2005 might just be Robin van Persie's year.

It was one of the goals of the season, one which would be replayed countless times from every possible angle. Coincidentally, this match took place around six months into van Persie's first season with Arsenal; Wenger had said it usually took players six months to adapt to life in the Premier League.

When Arsenal played the return fixture at Southampton in February they had both Bergkamp and Reyes suspended following an ill-mannered FA Cup tie with Sheffield United. It was up to Henry and van Persie to lead the line against the strugglers. Things were going to plan when David Prutton was dismissed for Southampton before Ljungberg put the Gunners 1-0 up. Van Persie was lucky to escape with just a yellow card in the first half as he appeared to elbow Rory Delap in the face. This elbow did not go unnoticed and was his second such offence in December (as Sir Alex Ferguson would tell anybody who would listen). Wenger warned van Persie to calm down at half-time but he completely lost his head after the break and a rash challenge on Graeme Le Saux drew a second yellow card to level up the numbers.

Van Persie had told Arsenal TV that every proper footballer was 'his own piece of art', but with a performance like that he was more a badly scrawled imitation Banksy than the Mona Lisa.

As he trudged off the field, van Persie felt the full wrath of Arsène Wenger who could not believe what he had just seen. Later on, Wenger told the *People*: 'What did I say when van Persie went past me? I just told him he'd had his warning. I told him at half-time he'd been booked already and with the home side down to 10 men, the referee might be looking to make another quick booking to even things up. Van Persie had his chance to calm down, he had his chance to keep cool and to think about what he had to do – and yet he still does something like that. I talked to him afterwards but what I said will remain private.'

Southampton took full advantage of an Arsenal defensive mishap when 6 foot 7 inch striker Peter Crouch used his height to make it look easy as he headed home from goalkeeper Jens Lehmann's flapped clearance to tie the game.

Southampton manager Harry Redknapp said this was a 'bonus point' for his side but Arsenal desperately needed to pick up all three at St. Mary's and now lagged ten points behind Chelsea, who also had the luxury of a game in hand. Like a doting father at his child's school parents evening, whether they had done right or wrong, Wenger always sided with his players in post-match interviews. But this game proved to be the exception to the rule as the finger was firmly pointed at the man who was sent off. With Reyes and Bergkamp missing, van Persie was desperately needed, not only in this game but for upcoming fixtures, but now he too would have to spend time out serving a suspension.

Wenger had even warned van Persie at half-time that he was treading on thin ice but his advice had apparently fallen on deaf ears. He fumed: 'I cannot support what van Persie did, he knew he had to behave himself. When you are playing against 10 men, the most important thing is to keep 11 players yourself. I told him at half-time that when the home team has a player sent off, the referee is under pressure to send off an opposing player who has already been booked. I am definitely not happy with his attitude and behaviour. We know he shouldn't have done it and he's intelligent enough to know. It was unprofessional. It is difficult to put yourself in his boots and explain his reactions. Intelligent behaviour is needed on the pitch to win big games.'

Southampton manager Harry Redknapp wasn't exactly full of praise for van Persie's actions either, branding him a 'stupid player' for what he saw as a needless red card. In a typically straight-talking interview, Redknapp said: 'Luckily they had a stupid player on their side as well and he obviously decided he was going to get himself sent off to make it a fairer game for us.'

Freddie Ljungberg stopped short of saying van Persie had let Arsenal down but said they desperately needed his creative presence on the pitch. He told the *Sun*: 'I wouldn't say Robin has let the side down but we're all disappointed with the sending off. We had an opportunity to play with 11 men against 10 and we didn't use that advantage at all. We specifically spoke about it at half-time, the need to be careful and not get any more silly yellow cards. But within five minutes of the second half we're down to 10 men as well. I'm sure the boss will speak to him. There's no question that he has talent but we need him on the pitch and today we missed him for the last 35 minutes.'

He was being condemned left, right and centre but finally someone came out to defend van Persie – team mate Ashley Cole admitted he had committed similar crimes in the past and insisted the Dutchman could put the incident behind him. Cole told the *Evening Standard*: 'Robin hasn't let anyone down. I've done it before and I hope nobody blamed me. It's something that can happen in the spur of the moment.'

That sending off at Southampton came at exactly the wrong time as Arsenal were already desperately short up front. At the time it may have seemed that Wenger's very public criticism spelled trouble but perhaps that was the worst of what was said to van Persie and the two could move on quickly. Much like a bust up in a relationship, it was probably a lot easier to get on with things with everything out in the open than if Wenger had said nothing at all.

As well as harsh words for van Persie in public, there was a private line of dialogue going on with his manager. Wenger loved playing mind games with the opposition but it seems he also had a penchant for trying it on his own players.

Van Persie told the *Independent*: 'He didn't shout or say I was wrong. He just opened up a question,' the player recalls. 'He said, "If you want to go to the top level, you have to change something." I said, "Okay, what?" He said,

"I'm not telling you, find out for yourself." So I went away and asked myself what I wanted from football. The manager was very clever. He thought if he told me what I needed I might forget it in one week, but if I figured it out myself, maybe it would take longer, but it would stay in my mind. I matured. I decided from then on I'd do everything to be successful, go to training and watch how the older players do it, become a lot more professional than before.'

Van Persie was mentally strong following years of playing street football in Rotterdam. He had played on the harsh concrete streets from when he was first allowed out of the house on his own right up until his breakthrough into the first team at Feyenoord. Playing in the baking Kralingen streets in a 'winner stays on' competition taught him how to handle pressure and stay mentally strong during stressful periods. Practising regularly was the only way to become a great footballer according to van Persie and the intense 'winner stays on' matches fought out on the streets of Rotterdam had given him plenty of opportunity to learn how to play the game.

Street football can be extremely unforgiving for a young teenager with no referee in sight and the popular kids' mates lining the sides of the pitch (a bit like those Ajax fans) just waiting to squirt their water bottles or stick out a leg. That street football bred the mental strength that helped van Persie make it in the game – the driving force as he made it through the darkness that was the end of his Feyenoord career and into the piercing sunlight of Highbury stadium.

That environment was the breeding ground for a lot of talent as van Persie said a total of seven professional footballers grew up within three streets of each other in

Kralingen. His best friend, Ajax's Nouredine Boukhari, was one of them.

He told the *Independent*: 'There were lots of better players than me. They were fantastic with the ball, with fantastic tricks. I know a lot of guys who were brilliant but not strong enough in the mind. When I go back to Holland, they say, "I should have taken my chance. You took it and I'm proud of you." And I say, "You were 10 times better than me but you messed up." If you want to make it in football you have to take your chances and be patient.'

It was strange for a man red-carded for a needless tackle to boast of his patience and this may have been a false claim for van Persie to make about himself. From that St. Mary's lunge right through a World Cup Final yellow card, van Persie would consistently show an impatient character throughout his career. Perhaps this interview was his attempt at turning a corner. It didn't quite work, but nice try.

Indeed it was largely thanks to those daily pilgrimages to the city streets that van Persie's great left foot had developed from his tame secondary weapon into a trusty sniper rifle. Every footballer tells young hopefuls that practice is the key to success and the proof was in the pudding that former Netherlands coach Marco van Basten had gone on to call it a 'great left foot'.

In what sounded a bit like a training video, he said: 'My left foot is because of the street. In the beginning it was poor. When I was eight, nine, ten, it was nothing. I didn't realise that it was good for me. But I like the game so I shot and shot and shot. Goal after goal.'

That honest and frank nature was a breath of fresh air because van Persie had clearly been reflecting back on what had got him this far in his career. He certainly had his feet more firmly planted on the ground than your typical player who invested the entirety of their spare time in video gaming and getting up to no good in nightclubs and hotel rooms. More on that later.

Arsenal strikers were thin on the ground and van Persie was called upon when Ljungberg was injured in the warm-up before their game at Blackburn Rovers nearly a month later. Their title dreams were already effectively over as they sat 13 points adrift of leaders Chelsea with Henry, Bergkamp and Pires all missing. But van Persie took the game by the scruff of the neck and hit the only goal of the game just before the break. Left-back Cole, the only man to defend van Persie after the red mist came down on the south coast, threaded an inch-perfect pass through to the Dutchman who spun majestically away from his man and snuck around Brad Friedel to tap home. Only the woodwork could deny him a second goal after the American goalkeeper was unable to get anywhere near an absolute peach of a left-footed curler. Playing in a young side shorn of four of the club's biggest names, van Persie went some way towards paying back his boss for that howler at Southampton.

This was an unexpected boost for Wenger who must have feared the worst before kick-off. He purred to the Sky cameras afterwards: 'It was a positive game and overall I feel we created the best chances. Van Persie was not due to start but he's shown that he can play and he took his chance well today. We have experienced players in our side but if you look at how we were today with the young side, when they all come back together it will be an interesting squad.'

Van Persie was over the moon that his first goal in months had taken Arsenal back up to second place in the table. Clearly in a jubilant mood, he told Sky shortly after the game: 'I am very happy because we have won and got second place and I scored, my last goal came two months ago. It was a hard time for me after Southampton because I got a red card and it was stupid. But that was then and it's been a great day for me. It was a hard month and I've trained hard and I'm happy today. We were an unbelievably young side but I think we played very well. Mentally this win will help us for the FA Cup semi-final.'

It was all well and good for him to come out after the Southampton shambles and say he had been stupid but it was clear the Dutch ace thought this put water between himself and that incident. In scoring an important goal when his team mates looked out of ideas, he had gone some way to appease Wenger and the Highbury faithful. The post-match comment showed that although he was still having those hot-head moments, he was starting to grow up.

That FA Cup semi-final was massive for Arsenal because it was their only chance to get their hands on some silverware that season as they were already out of the running to retain their Premier League crown. After some of the older members of that 'Invincibles' squad had been put out to graze, the new kids who came in had not been up to the same high standard. Van Persie was still very much seen as 'one for the future' but winning the world's most famous domestic cup competition would not be a bad way to get the ball rolling.

Traditionally the FA Cup final was always played at Wembley Stadium, with the semi-finals at large club grounds such as Sheffield Wednesday's Hillsborough and Aston Villa's Villa Park. With the historic Wembley stadium being rebuilt, the Football Association was in a state of flux at the start of the century. Finals were switched to the Football Association of Wales' impressive Millennium Stadium in Cardiff and in 2005 both semi-finals were also played in the Welsh capital.

In the league, Arsenal had cruised to a 3-0 win at Blackburn in August and van Persie's goal had given them a 1-0 win in the return fixture at Ewood Park, so it came as little surprise that the Gunners were seen as firm favourites to make the final. Mark Hughes had the Lancashire club playing a brand of effective, if mean, football that made them a potential banana skin for this notoriously delicate Arsenal side. As Thierry Henry missed the game through injury, this was José Antonio Reyes' chance to cement a place in the side as van Persie could only look on from the substitutes' bench.

Robert Pires' first-half strike looked to have a win in the bag but things remained edgy as this icy encounter drew to a close. The Frenchman netted from close range in a largely disappointing semi-final. The stadium was below capacity and Blackburn flooded the midfield to stop Arsenal from going about things in their usual attractive manner. Referee Steve Dunn booked three Rovers men in a brutal first half. It had been a frustrating afternoon of thumb-twiddling for van Persie, who finally found his way onto the pitch when he replaced Bergkamp after 82 minutes. He only had a few minutes to make his mark but within four minutes van Persie had made the game safe for his side with a stunning solo goal.

Lucas Neill was left in no-man's land by a trademark Dutch turn as he spun away from the Australian before charging towards the Blackburn goal. He knew exactly what to do as the big American goalkeeper Brad Friedel charged off his line in an attempt to close the angle – van Persie got a shot away early before anybody had a moment to intervene, stroking the ball past Friedel and into the bottom right-hand corner of the net. Pires ran over to embrace the goalscorer as he raised his arms aloft in front of the Arsenal faithful, who went wild with celebration after such a brilliant goal. Game over? Not quite yet.

It got even better for Robin in the 90th minute after Pires had broken away into space down the left-hand side of the expansive Millennium Stadium pitch. He did well to pick out the centre forward who swept home with a first-time effort. The ball crept just inside the post to make this a much more emphatic victory than it could have been and van Persie had really proved himself.

He may have only been on the pitch for eight minutes but van Persie somehow managed to steal the show. Just seven short weeks after his red card at Southampton, van Persie had gone from zero to hero.

But the course of this man's life never runs smoothly and after his second goal touched the back of the net, Blackburn hard man Andy Todd ran into the scorer, who suffered a bloodied lip as a result. He wasn't seriously injured but it was just typical that something had to go wrong – Todd's flailing elbow the only downside of a fantastic afternoon's work for the Dutchman.

After the game there was an outcry over Todd's elbow and for a while he became public enemy number one. His reputation took a dive as hacks labelled him 'The Butcher of Blackburn', yet following a thorough investigation, the FA cleared him of violent conduct and said the collision had been an accident.

Todd was a family man who shied away from the public eye but in the months that followed, he was so harshly criticised that the big defender saw fit to clear his name. He told the *Mirror*: 'As you can see, it was a pure accident. When you freeze it at the moment of impact, look where my arm is. I turned to go back to the centre circle and he ran into my shoulder. Robin's looking at the ball and I'm looking at the ball. He ran into me. I apologised to the Arsenal players straight away. Some accepted my apology and others didn't.

'I looked in the papers the next day and the pictures looked awful. They chose the worst ones. I even started doubting myself. I thought, "Have I done it?" But, as you can see, there was no forearm smash or even elbow. It was an accident.'

Arsène Wenger complained to the *Sun* after the game: 'Van Persie's sending-off at Southampton was the turning point. Until then, he was going nowhere in the way he approached the game. Since then he has changed – I hope for ever. There has never been any doubt about his talent but he was flashy and that got him sent off against Southampton.

'How has he changed? The great players respect the game and do what the game wants. He wasn't always doing that. Sometimes it's more difficult to do that when you have a big talent. You know you can do the little trick that is not necessarily needed. But now, for him, the game comes first and van Persie second.'

This was classic post-match twaddle from Wenger – van Persie had come on and scored two goals in eight minutes and apparently he only cares about the game and not himself? Surely the aim of every striker is to kick the football into the goal as many times as possible. Wenger once again likened him to a young Dennis Bergkamp – the man he replaced and managed to outshine in just eight minutes.

They were never going to catch Chelsea in the title race but Arsenal finished strongly under pressure from Manchester United, going on to score 14 more goals before the end of the season.

Van Persie put in an unremarkable performance as Arsenal beat Tottenham 1-0 to complete a Premier League double over their bitter rivals. When relegation-threatened West Bromwich Albion made the trip to Highbury with just two more games remaining to scramble for Premier League survival, they found van Persie back to his menacing best. Wenger fielded a relatively youthful Arsenal side but it was certainly one capable of delivering the goods.

After Zoltan Gera had threatened for the visitors, van Persie flexed his muscles with a ferocious volley just before the break, which was only just kept out by an excellent Russell Hoult save. The goalkeeper could do nothing in the 66th minute when Reyes played an inviting ball for van Persie, who cut inside defender Neil Clement to bury with that left foot. West Brom brought on three strikers – including former Gunner Nwankwo Kanu – in a desperate attempt to salvage something from the game but Arsenal exploited the gaps left to make it 2-0. Edu converted Dennis Bergkamp's pass to ensure that West Brom – who would eventually stay up on a dramatic final day of the season – went home empty handed.

Arsenal warmed up for that FA Cup final appearance in fine style with a 7-0 demolition of Everton in their final home game of the season. The Merseysiders went into the game with a goal difference of plus seven but that was completely wiped out when they were steamrolled at Highbury. Van Persie got the ball rolling with less than ten minutes gone before Pires (2), Vieira, Edu, Bergkamp and Mathieu Flamini all joined in the fun.

It was a defence-splitting pass from Bergkamp – rumoured to be leaving the club and his young apprentice behind at the end of the season – that set up van Persie to kick off proceedings. The 36-year-old played a ball right through the middle of David Weir and Joseph Yobo and his countryman gratefully put the chance away.

Arsenal were apparently reluctant to offer Bergkamp – out of contract at the end of the season – a year's extension. He played his socks off and the supporters housed in the Clock End shared their thoughts on the matter with chants of 'one more year!'. Bergkamp leaving the club at this stage would have had a detrimental effect on van Persie – he would be better served by learning from the master for a few more seasons before emerging from his shadows just yet.

To the relief of player and supporters alike, it was announced in the lead up to the FA Cup final that Bergkamp was to stay for another year . The Dutch duo would be together for another season at least. Patrick Vieira knew how important it was for van Persie's future that Bergkamp was to stay for another season. After the FA Cup final he said: 'It is very important for us because with

Dennis' experience all the young players coming through – Reyes, van Persie and the others – can learn from him.'

When it was revealed that the talismanic Henry was to miss the final, the stage looked set for van Persie to start in his place. This would have been a massive opportunity for him to shine and he must have been gutted when it was announced that Reyes was to start instead. He had managed to steal the show in just eight minutes in the semi-final but Manchester United were in no mood to allow him to do the same when van Persie was brought on for Cesc Fàbregas with 86 minutes played. Paul Scholes had gone close with a header and Arsenal stopper Jens Lehmann had to be smart to block Wayne Rooney's drive as United ran the show for most of the game. Wayne Rooney and Ruud van Nistelrooy both rattled the woodwork late in the second half as United pushed for what would have been a deserved victory.

If Arsenal were having a few technical difficulties it was nothing compared to the Millennium Stadium roof, which was designed to close out adverse weather conditions but was stuck open and could not stop the rain from hammering down onto the greasy pitch.

Arsenal looked as flat as a pancake and nothing could separate the two sides, so the game headed into 30 minutes of extra time. It summed up how poorly his side were playing that when van Persie drew a smart save from Roy Carroll with a free-kick at the start of extra time, he had registered his side's first shot on target in the entire game. The menacing figure of van Persie triggered a state of panic in the United defence – Mikael Silvestre lunging horribly for the ball to give away that free-kick. The substitute was desperate to recreate his semi-final heroics but the Northern

Irish goalkeeper was equal to another van Persie effort as time ticked away.

Reyes had a moment of madness and was sent off at the end of the 30 minutes for elbowing Cristiano Ronaldo. It seemed a strange decision not to start van Persie and after an ineffective game, Reyes thanked his manager by drawing that red card. Those fresh legs couldn't make a difference and the two famous rivals could not be separated by 120 minutes of football. For the first time in the competition's history it was to go down to a penalty shoot-out to decide who would take the cup home. The pressure was on with English players in particular having a well-documented history of failure when games were to be decided this way – the national side had been sent out of World Cups and European Championships on penalty kicks.

This situation was exactly the kind that van Persie dealt with well – the pressure was piled on every man stepping up to take a kick and the eyes of the world were on him. There were no problems as he smashed the ball into the top left-hand corner to keep Arsenal's noses in front after Lehmann had blocked Paul Scholes' effort. All the other penalties went in, meaning Arsenal had won the FA Cup 5-4 on penalties. His toil on the pitch during open play might not have resulted in a goal but van Persie's spot kick had helped ensure the cup went back to Highbury and the side won a trophy in his debut season.

Brazilian star Edu had been set to take one of the penalties but backed out at the last minute to give van Persie the chance to step up. He might not have taken a penalty for Arsenal before but the 20-year-old was the kind of player who would swim rather than sink when faced with such a challenge. The way he speedily volunteered to step into the breach showed Wenger just how keen van Persie was to prove himself and be of worth to Arsenal.

He told the *Birmingham Evening Mail*: 'Edu went to the coach and said he was not confident about taking his penalty and I said, "I am, I want to take it." The boss said, "OK you can." I may not have looked nervous but I really was, my legs were shaking.'

Those legs may have been shaking but he left Roy Carroll no chance with a spot-kick high into the corner of the net. It was a fantastic moment for van Persie to keep his nerve and show that Steve Rowley had made the correct call; the Dutchman clearly thrived in high-pressure situations. Patrick Vieira, the man so often involved in controversies between the sides in recent seasons, scored the winning spot-kick and said it took mental strength to win on penalties.

There were scenes of jubilation from the lucky Arsenal players, who must have counted themselves extremely fortunate to have been taking the cup home after being dominated from start to finish by the Old Trafford side.

Wenger also hailed the mentality of the players, who he admitted had not been the better side in the 120 minutes. He said: 'United created four great chances and they played well. We won it with our mental strength and resilience rather than the usual style. It's important to go back with the trophy even though we could have played better.'

This is where the addition of van Persie had been so positive for the Gunners. That history of growing up playing Rotterdam street football and surviving bitter encounters with rivals Ajax had produced a man who would not be trembling at the thought of a high-pressure spot-kick. The fact that Reyes had dealt with the pressure by getting himself sent off in the 120th minute could only benefit van Persie and put him ahead of the Spaniard in Wenger's eyes when the next season came around.

Despite his Dutch heritage van Persie said that the FA Cup win meant a lot to him. Looking back on the triumph, he said: 'We won the FA Cup last season and that was big for me as well because everyone in Holland knows how great a competition it is. But the Premiership is big as well and I want to win it. There is a big belief among the players that we can catch Chelsea and win it.'

His first season in English football had certainly been memorable, one in which van Persie's name had been on the lips of pundits and supporters – if not always for the right reasons. The peaks of that cup win and scoring in that Highbury record Champions League win would be balanced out by the troughs of the St Mary's red card and that M25 car smash. He had achieved a lot and was clearly hungry to progress further in the Champions League and lift the Premier League trophy.

It was far from perfect, but at such a tender age, it would have been unrealistic to expect him to be the finished product yet. Van Persie was still very much a player in development and, with Arsène Wenger clearly having his sights set on the long term rather than chasing instant results at any cost, where better to do that than Arsenal? The Gunners knew what they were taking on when they rescued him from Rotterdam – a rough diamond to be polished and incorporated into their crown of a squad.

By the tremendously high standards that had been set the previous season, this had not been a brilliant campaign for the Gunners, but van Persie had still managed to get his hands on one of the most famous cups in world football. Furthermore, his two important goals in the semi-final victory over Blackburn had been vital to the team's progression to the final.

That esteemed sorcerer Dennis Bergkamp – one of the most gifted players in the history of Dutch football – was ready and willing to pass on his knowledge to the young apprentice. It was also great for van Persie to have a compatriot close by who had his back. Had it not been for 'The Ice Man' stepping in to reason with police officers after that car crash, the scenario could have played out very differently and it is worth noting that leaving the scene of a crash after damaging the central reservation barrier – as van Persie hastily did – is a crime that could be severely punished by a judge on a bad day.

Arsenal went to great lengths to make sure their foreign imports were properly settled in their newly-adopted country, and that 'after-care' service certainly played its part as van Persie quickly found his feet in England. The lives of players at other clubs were mostly attended to by their agents but when they took the initiative themselves, Arsenal were stealing a march and their new recruits would deliver the goods sooner than perhaps they would have at other clubs. Cesc Fàbregas certainly looked nicely settled after joining a few months before van Persie – he made useful contributions to the side and delivered performances way beyond his eighteen years.

It was turning out to be quite a year for van Persie as he

made his debut for the full Netherlands squad at the start of June 2005. The national coach was not exactly a stranger to van Persie: former AC Milan and Ajax star Marco van Basten. When van Persie had been waiting for Arsenal to rescue him from Feyenoord and he was attacked by Ajax supporters, van Basten was the man who had jumped in the way of the thugs and saved him a real beating and the possibility of serious injury.

After picking the Arsenal star, van Basten hailed Arsène Wenger for salvaging van Persie from the Feyenoord scrapheap and breathing new life into his nation's wayward talent. He had been almost forgotten in his year away from the Netherlands after having once been tipped as the nation's hottest emerging talent. This was to be the start of a long-running love-in between van Persie's two managers, who would keep each other updated with the odd text message about what the players had been up to.

Johan Cruyff was easily the country's most famous footballer after he starred in the Netherlands' famous 'Total Football' side in the 1970s. The word of Cruyff was never questioned and he had said van Persie was the hottest young talent when he emerged at Feyenoord. That early promise had been forgotten by many in the Netherlands but van Basten had kept tabs on the fallen prince.

Ahead of van Persie's debut the former AC Milan star said: 'Robin has been brilliant and amazing in training and is completely changed from how he was. You can see the difference from how he was last year and he has benefited from being at Arsenal. He has learned a lot under Arsène Wenger and playing with exceptional players.

'He had a bad reputation in Holland with Feyenoord

because his attitude was too casual, but he is now showing he has exceptional qualities and is going to be a great player. He realised at Arsenal that if he is not professional and toes the line, he will be on the sidelines and it will be the end of his career. He has picked up the message. He is very good and will be an asset for the Dutch team. I am happy with his progress and I am very positive.'

The professionalism instilled in the Arsenal players by Wenger had obviously impressed van Basten. This had been a culture change for van Persie and it was one that had certainly had a positive effect on his career. He would pick and choose who to respect and Wenger was certainly a man who gave and received respect. Young players can prosper when a father figure is present and Wenger performed that role with van Persie. Tough love had often been the order of the day but sometimes that is the most effective way for a father to act.

Robin van Persie's international debut came on 4 June 2005 when he came off the bench with the side cruising to a 2-0 World Cup qualifying win over Romania. He came on for Ruud van Nistelrooy just after the hour mark and was keen to make an impression with the half hour he was given. It was almost a debut to remember when Arjen Robben set him up perfectly, but van Persie's effort skidded wide of the post with the goalkeeper scrambling across goal. It was hard to make a mark with the win already in the bag and minds already drifting to a trip to Finland in just a few days.

It would have been understandable for van Persie to have a bit of a chip on his shoulder playing alongside Robben for the national team. When the pair were teenagers, Johan Cruyff had singled out van Persie as the better of the two and later labelled him the country's 'best youngster in a generation'. But after that falling-out with van Marwijk, van Persie had only been able to command a transfer fee of £2.75 million whereas Robben was sold by his club PSV Eindhoven for £12 million. After the way things had worked out at Feyenoord, van Persie was made to look like an inferior player and could have gone out wanting to prove a point to his 'more valuable' countryman.

Four days later he was given an even shorter window of opportunity when brought on for van Nistelrooy with 75 minutes played as the Netherlands led 1-0 in Finland. His Manchester United nemesis had put the Dutch ahead with a close-range effort but it was only with the introduction of van Persie that the Netherlands really got going.

After combining well with Robben, the new man in the team cleverly presented Dirk Kuyt with an open goal to double the lead. Van Persie was actually bearing down on the goal himself but chose to lay the ball back with the goalkeeper haring off his line. He had only been on the pitch a matter of minutes but things got even better shortly afterwards. Van Persie did brilliantly to keep the ball from crossing the touchline and the Finns had no answer for his mesmerising step-overs. Before anybody could get a foot on the ball he had crossed for Philip Cocu to prod home a third.

This emphatic introduction to the international scene was complete when he thundered through the ragged Finland defence to sweep home his first goal for the Netherlands. After nodding a header into the path of Kuyt, van Persie received the ball back instantly and his pace was too much for the tired Finns as he lashed the ball into the far corner of the net. It was a fantastic night for van Persie, who had become something of a hate figure towards the end of his Feyenoord days but showed the Dutch public what he was all about in an outstanding 15-minute cameo appearance.

He gleefully ran to the Orange army housed on the side of the pitch with arms aloft before turning around and pointing at the name on the back of his shirt. He was mobbed by team mates and coach Marco van Basten applauded from the technical area. Supporters chanted his name as the final whistle blew – not many players have had such a big impact in their second game for their country and most would be trialled in friendly matches before being trusted with competitive games. Van Persie had done brilliantly when thrown in at the deep end and put himself in with a shot of getting into the squad for the World Cup in Germany the next summer. The team just needed to get there first.

Van Basten did not heap too much praise on his new recruit in the post-match press conference; instead fellow substitute Hedwiges Maduro was talked up and the coach said his team had been better than Finland. He did later say that van Persie had matured in his first Premier League season – having left the Eredivisie under something of a cloud.

Understandably, van Persie was beaming after an incredible 15-minute appearance. He said: 'I feel fantastic, I played 15 minutes and got two assists and a goal. I'm very happy. Now we can prepare for the tournament in Germany.'

It was time for van Persie to reflect on the season that had begun in troubled fashion but ended victoriously in Cardiff and Helsinki. He might not have had as clean a run in a side in his professional career as he may have wanted, but van

Persie had still managed to collect UEFA Cup and FA Cup winners medals in that time. He had gatecrashed the Netherlands side and might even have muscled his way into their World Cup finals squad with an impressive start on the international scene.

Arsenal's title challenge had faded after they had been so dominant in the previous season and it was clear that Wenger had some wheeling and dealing to be getting on with that summer. It was hard to tell how these changes would work out for van Persie; would he be playing as part of a more successful team or would he be forced out of the picture by a fresh face? He already faced stiff competition from José Antonio Reyes but the cup final (Reyes' red and van Persie's penalty) might have sealed his place as third choice behind Thierry Henry and Dennis Bergkamp. A good 2005/2006 season could see him take over the mantle from Bergkamp and become a regular starter for the Gunners.

Things were going well, so it was inevitable that he wanted to remain at Highbury for as long as possible. He told the *People* that time away from the club had made him realise how brilliantly things had gone in that first season: 'Marco van Basten was right to say I have developed as a player. I am very happy with myself and my position at Arsenal and Holland. I can see myself staying at Arsenal for many years. My contract has another three years to run and of course we will have to see about it. I can learn a lot from Dennis Bergkamp and it is great he has signed a new contract. He is a fantastic player. It's very important for a young player to play regularly. The last two or three months I played a lot for Arsenal.'

CHAPTER 3

CRISIS TIME

It had been a long hard season but finally van Persie had a few weeks to relax before joining up with his Arsenal colleagues for pre-season training. He told Dutch journalists he would have a break with Bouchra to get away from the stress that had built up over the past year. He reasoned: 'I have had so many things to cope with. In one year I have got married, moved abroad, made my debut for Arsenal, made my debut for Holland. I feel really stressed.'

He was riding on the crest of a wave and had understandably been out with his international team mates to celebrate the fact they were top of their qualifying group. Spirits were high and unfortunately van Persie's jubilation was to be cut short. When people are stressed they sometimes do things they normally wouldn't – something Robin and Bouchra were about to learn first-hand.

That hate-tarnished trip back to Amsterdam the previous summer would not exactly have been a treasured memory for van Persie but this visit to his native land was to turn out a hundred times worse. On Monday 13 June 2005, Robin van Persie was arrested on suspicion of rape. This was an extremely serious matter and a massive question mark hung over his Arsenal future as supporters anxiously awaited details of what had happened.

He was arrested and held after an incident alleged to have happened in Rotterdam over the weekend. A spokeswoman for the prosecutor's office told the BBC: 'Robin van Persie was arrested on Monday suspected of a rape incident that took place at the weekend. We cannot reveal any details of what happened as the Dutch legal system is different to that in England.'

If found guilty, van Persie could have been jailed for a maximum of 12 years. It was confirmed that he would be held in custody. He was forced to spend time in Noordsingel Jail, which was over 100 years old and badly overcrowded. The Dutch public had given him enough grief out on the streets in the last few months; things could only get worse if he had to mix with the country's criminals. He would have come across Ajax supporters in jail and without Marco van Basten there to obstruct them, his life would surely become a daily battle.

Former Arsenal hero Tony Adams famously served two months of a four-month jail sentence in the early 1990s after admitting to drink-driving offences. Van Persie had not been under the influence at the time of his earlier car crash but that might still have been a blot on his character during the trial. That previous offence was picked up by the media and van Persie was in danger of a judge latching onto the 'bad boy' image that had followed him around for several years.

Things were different at Arsenal before Arsène Wenger took charge in 1996: players were well known for a 'pub culture' that saw members of the squad have brushes with the law. Adams, the centre back who would go on to captain club and country, was apparently handcuffed to a Tottenham-supporting inmate whilst being transported to prison. The Spurs fan apparently moaned: 'What a nightmare. I'm a Tottenham fan and I get cuffed to you.' A convicted Ajax fan might have had slightly stronger words in store for former Feyenoord star van Persie.

Abraham Moszkowicz, van Persie's lawyer, told Dutch television he believed the Arsenal star would soon be released for lack of evidence. He said: 'I know the class of the young lady concerned – how I can't tell you – and I put large question marks around the truth content of her story.'

Dutch national under-21 coach Foppe de Haan, who had guided the star through his formative years to his selection for the full international team earlier in the month, told Dutch news agency ANP: 'It was quite a shock to me to hear about it and it makes me a bit sad, but let's not judge or condemn too quickly.'

The offence was alleged to have taken place in a hotel room van Persie and two friends had visited during a night out on Saturday 11 June. Twenty-two-year-old half-Dutch, half-Nigerian Sandra Boma Krijgsman claimed she had gone back to a hotel with van Persie after the pair had chatted in the city's Baja Beach nightclub. Krijgsman, who was a former stripper and pole dancer, according to the *Sun*, claimed she was groped in the hotel room before being forced into the bathroom and raped.

Moszkowicz said that after a 45-minute jail cell

discussion, the player had denied having had sexual intercourse with the woman after spending the night in several upmarket bars in Rotterdam including the famous cocktail joint Hyper Hyper.

Arsène Wenger was in court on the Tuesday but not to help van Persie – he had to appear at the High Court to give evidence on behalf of Atlético Mineiro – the former club of another Arsenal player, Brazilian Gilberto Silva, in a case they were fighting against two agents. These were stressful times for Wenger, who should have been spending time reflecting on the season that had been but instead had the headache of two players involved in legal proceedings.

After he had been in prison for the Dutch legal maximum of three days without charge, van Persie would have been hoping to be released. But things were to go from bad to worse with the prosecution team successfully appealing for more time in order to investigate further. Arsenal had remained quiet on the matter but surely discussions were being conducted in the Highbury boardroom to decide how the club would react to the different possible outcomes of the proceedings.

A prosecution spokeswoman said: 'We asked the judge for a longer custody, for 14 days, and he granted it. The public prosecutors' office has asked for the custody to be prolonged in the interest of the investigation and because of the seriousness of the charges.'

Abraham Moszkowicz, van Persie's lawyer, was still adamant van Persie did not have sexual contact, consensual or otherwise, with the former beauty queen. He told reporters: 'He denies he had any sexual contact with this girl. Nothing happened.'

In those two weeks locked in a cell, van Persie must have thought about the unthinkable – what would happen if he was convicted and spent time in jail? In a matter of weeks he had gone from lifting the FA Cup and starring in an orange shirt to languishing in prison. A return to Highbury and the planned pre-season tours seemed a million miles away as he sat locked in prison. There was a possibility of the period he could be held without charge being extended to four months. This would have a serious impact on van Persie's preparation for what was meant to be his breakthrough season.

To go from the pampered lifestyle of a top-flight footballer to living in a cell in a matter of days would obviously be a shock to the system. Once the ordeal was over, van Persie described the full horror of his prison nightmare. Items were thrown at him and inevitably people shouted 'rapist'. He said: 'The prisoners were bringing the house down with their shouting. They were like wild animals in a cage. The prison warden, who took me to my cell, said he had been there for seven years and never seen anything like it. I had to undergo all that because of the false accusations of one woman.'

Those fellow inmates kicked off so badly that guards had no option but to place van Persie in solitary confinement in order to avoid any compromise to his safety. It must have been a culture shock to go from the plush suburban home he shared with Bouchra to a 7x12 foot cell with a toilet in the corner. He was prevented from making any contact with the outside world and it would have been very easy to lose heart. A passing prison warden's comment that van Persie's career with Arsenal and the Netherlands was over proved to be a turning point.

Van Persie said: 'OK, so the whole world thinks I am finished. Well, that was the turning point. That really motivated me to come out as a strong person. I thought, "I will show you here who is the strongest." And I knew that if and when I came out of that hell, I would be mentally strong enough to become a big player.'

He had been psychologically strengthened by this rough period and having been through that prison hell and the agony of not knowing how long he would be kept inside for, it would take a lot to upset him in the future.

To make matters worse, a woman came forward to tell the press she had seen the star up to no good shortly before the alleged incident took place. She did not have too much to add to the story but it was clear the newspapers would gobble up any scraps thrown to them to keep the narrative of the story going. It was alleged that van Persie had been flirting with two women in a Rotterdam nightclub in which waitresses wore bikinis.

Nathalie Vroegindeweii, 20, told the *Sun*: 'I saw him at the bar with two girls. He was being touchy-feely, but not in an inappropriate way, just flirty.'

Defending was not van Persie's speciality on the pitch but surely his high-profile lawyer had enough experience in the courtroom to know that he should have stuck to his original story. By Friday 17 June, Moszkowicz confirmed van Persie had been in a room at the £70 a night Tulip hotel – round the corner from his penthouse apartment where Bouchra was sleeping – with two of his friends and the girl. When asked what van Persie was planning to do as he went to the hotel with the girl, the defence lawyer said maybe he was going to play football.

Former Dutch Miss Universe and Miss Nigeria winner Krijgsman had claimed one of the players hid the black mini-skirt and shirt she was wearing.

Moszkowicz said in a statement: 'What I can tell you is that she met two people after what she is calling the rape, but she did not tell them that my client raped her or even mention the name of my client. She was only saying that someone had played a kind of joke on her and stole her clothes.

'She was upset and not amused. If someone is raped and you talk immediately after with two persons, you would ask for the police to be called but she did not do this. She was only upset because of the fact that someone took her clothes. She stated she was raped and stated how it was done. I cannot tell you any details.'

Moszkowicz had been adamant van Persie did not have sexual contact with the woman but this had now had been downgraded to 'I cannot comment about whether he had sex or not.'

As the legal team sought to discredit the girl and say she was 'not the Queen of England', they were not doing the greatest job for van Persie with an inconsistent story. Bouchra was reportedly still standing by her man but he was now admitting to being in a hotel with a former stripper and surely this was not good for their marital relations.

On Saturday 18 June, the *Daily Star* awarded van Persie its 'Plonker of the Week' award and said that, although they were not saying he was guilty of anything, he had put himself in a position to cause more controversy and had to learn to keep out of potentially troublesome situations.

The next day Krijgsman broke her relative silence to

complain that the defence team was out to blacken her name by making things up and that she was not a nightclub dancer; she said her studies had been financed by modelling work.

Krijgsman told the *Sun*: 'He is trying to blacken my name as his only means of defence. I am certain about what happened and my only wish is to see justice done. I'm not a nightclub dancer of low esteem. What has been said is all wrong. I have spent several years studying tourism and training to be an air hostess.'

The defence team stuck to the story that the 22-year-old was angered by having her clothes hidden in a prank. They said: 'Let's say she feels she was not treated with the utmost respect. But knowing the reputation of the woman she damn well knew what she wanted when she decided to join van Persie and his friends at the hotel. She had certain reasons to join the group.'

With those allegations hanging over his head it was a lonely few days for van Persie. Not many people had come out and shown their support whilst he sat in limbo – spending time in a jail cell without having even been charged with a crime. The silence of Arsenal, his wife Bouchra and his father Bob would have done nothing to settle his nerves. Wenger later admitted to being worried about the youngster's future but at the time he remained tight-lipped.

The Dutch legal system operates extremely differently from the British system that says the accused are 'innocent until proven guilty'. Van Persie spent a total of two weeks behind bars fearing the worst and wondering what would happen if he were convicted.

Sports psychologist Wim Keizer told the *Sun* that some

players handle becoming an overnight success better than others, but that van Persie had football as the centre of his universe and said that was surprised he would be caught up in something like this: 'Robin has a complicated character, but there is nothing in his life but football. I am very shocked at what is alleged to have happened.'

When it came to talking about what might have happened in the hotel room, Bouchra was guarded. She trusted her man over a woman she did not know and it was clear that she just wanted the whole saga to draw to a conclusion. When she eventually did attend a court date, his understandably distraught wife left the room in tears before the judge even had a chance to make an announcement.

Bouchra said: 'I don't want to say anything about what might have happened in the hotel room. The only thing is that I trust Robin 200 per cent. I don't know this woman. And I don't want to know anything about her.'

She went on to explain that when she went out with her husband-to-be, girls would try it on with her man right under her nose. In an extremely mature statement, she claimed she knew what took place in nightclubs containing footballers but that she trusted her husband. Girls would see he was not interested and move on to the next star they laid their eyes on. She chirped that he would always flash his left hand showing a wedding band.

She said: 'I know exactly how it works in nightclubs like that. Whenever Robin and I went clubbing together women would throw themselves at him. It didn't make any difference that I was standing next to him. He would just laugh about it and show his wedding ring.'

Despite initially telling his lawyer that nothing happened

between himself and the former beauty queen, he would later go on to admit to sleeping with her. Bouchra had a choice – would she punish her cheating husband or would she forgive him?

Bouchra must have been heavily on the inmate's mind and he would have been wondering what would happen to his marriage when he got out. She was publicly backing his story, which suggested that the marriage would survive, but he would not find out what she truly felt until he was a free man.

Her parents had always warned Bouchra not to mix with van Persie in the early days but she had not listened to their pleas that he was trouble. Love aside, she would have had a much easier life staying with a multi-million earning footballer, even if she did have to paper over the cracks at times.

Sometimes it is incidents like this that turn boys into men. Indeed, when Wenger reflected back on the incident he said that van Persie emerged more mature and a stronger person for what he had come through. Perhaps in the long run the rape allegations made van Persie a stronger man as he was able to claw his way back from the brink and continue his life as normal. He had operated in the intense environments of derby matches in the Netherlands and England but this case was an entirely different kettle of fish.

If people are threatened with losing something they love, they cling to it tighter than ever before. In the same way that long lost supporters flock back to football clubs threatened with extinction, Bouchra could expect to be treated with more attention and respect from now on.

Several impressive displays had won Wenger around after that Southampton red card, but it would take more than a few romantic gestures to win his wife around after he cheated on her. The rape case put his infidelity very much in the public eye and that would have been a humiliating experience for Bouchra Elbali.

Newspaper talk that Arsène Wenger wanted to sign three players in the summer transfer window would have done nothing to reassure van Persie over his future at Arsenal. Hopefully when the Gunners were linked with a move for Real Madrid's attacking midfield ace Guti, van Persie was not informed.

On Wednesday 22 June, one of the two friends present in the hotel room on the night of the alleged incident spoke to the press. He claimed that Krijgsman had been making 'naughty suggestions' all night long and that the group thought they would see if she was true to her word.

The friend protested the Netherlands international's innocence but claimed the police would not listen to him because he was asleep at the time the incident was alleged to have taken place. He said: 'I believe Robin is innocent. I am absolutely certain. But when I tell the police, they say, "You were sleeping weren't you?"'

The unnamed friend, also a footballer, concurred with Bouchra's tales of van Persie having a lot of female attention to contend with whenever he was out on the town: 'The attention Robin gets from females in such places is enormous. It was early on a Sunday morning, we were leaning against the bar, and suddenly there she was. She stood almost up against him. She immediately started to talk to him. He reacted as he always does – very politely. We then went upstairs to have a quiet chat. We hadn't seen each other for a bit but it was like old times. Suddenly there's Sandra again. She whispered in his ear. She was being very cheeky and did not make it a secret that she wanted something from him.'

According to this account the former beauty queen was hardly the shyest of girls in the nightclub – if this was true she might have later regretted that attitude when her address became well known and she had a deluge of reporters knocking on her front door at all hours of the day. Things had become increasingly farcical in the hotel when the friends attempted to sit down and have a chat about football.

Van Persie's friend said: 'We were sitting on the sofa talking about football. We had the TV on. She suddenly started to yell. It was very odd. We looked up and saw that she had no trousers on. She said she had burned herself. A cigarette had dropped into her groin. She was probably not getting enough attention.'

As the two weeks of jail time reached their conclusion, Wenger sealed the signature of Stuttgart man Alexander Hleb in a £7 million deal. This would provide further competition for van Persie in an already congested squad.

In the days leading up to the trial, Arsenal finally threw their weight behind their player as vice-chairman David Dein and club solicitor Andrew Jolly spoke to Abraham Moszkowicz. It emerged that if van Persie was charged with rape at the hearing on Monday 27 June, his passport would be seized and retained by police in the months between the charge and the trial itself. This would prevent him from travelling back to England and joining up with the Arsenal squad for pre-season training and he would possibly miss the start of the Premier League season.

This meant that unless the court dropped the charges

completely, there was a realistic chance he might never play for Arsenal again. Wenger could not afford to wait around for months for a player and would surely find a replacement, leaving van Persie, who came to England with a poor reputation that had only been made worse by his behaviour on and off the pitch since joining the side.

Van Persie's lawyer remained optimistic and claimed new evidence would emerge at van Persie's showdown hearing that Monday: 'Arsenal are fully behind their player. They're supporting him very much. He is not allowed to read newspapers, speak to his family, friends or other prisoners. He is a high-profile player and draws incredible media attention. Police are concerned articles or TV programmes could affect their interviews.'

Feyenoord supporters turned up to protest on van Persie's behalf as they became concerned about his mental state.

One of the protesters, John van Leeuwen, told *Daily Mail* reporters: 'The prison is called the greenhouse because it gets so hot in there. Robin is only allowed a one-hour airing in a big cage. The rest of the day he is locked up. We are concerned about his mental state, because he has had to go through so much even before a court has decided whether he is guilty or not.'

He had left the Rotterdam club under a cloud but the supporters still came out to back their former star. It would have been understandable if the summer heat had been getting to him but hearing those gathered outside the prison block would have certainly raised his spirits. He was not allowed to read what was being said in the media so would not have been sure exactly what was being said about him. Hearing the supporters of his former team lend their backing would have kept hopes high of a release into a world that was not totally anti-Robin van Persie.

It was just as well that prison officers would not let their new inmate read the newspapers because the *Daily Express* printed a rather bleak picture on the day before that showdown. Cor Hellingman, a man who knew all about legal cases involving sports stars, speculated that on top of the extra three-month period van Persie could be held for without charge, he could then spend up to a year in jail waiting for the trial itself to take place.

It did depend on whether the court thought there was a risk he might re-offend or flee, and he might have been allowed to return to England in the meantime, but the risk was there. To a huge sigh of relief, the court released van Persie on Monday 27 June but worryingly did not clear his name.

A Justice Department spokeswoman said: 'He could still face prosecution. A decision about this will be taken later. The investigation still goes on, but it is not necessary to hold him any longer. There are no other restrictions imposed on him. He is free to go anywhere he wants.'

There were no bail terms imposed, which meant the ordeal was over for now and van Persie was free to join up with his club-mates on the arranged date of 19 July. He may have not been in top shape after spending weeks in a cramped cell with only an hour a day outside but the most important thing in the short-term was his freedom. He had certainly had an interesting summer holiday and would no doubt be the butt of jokes from colleagues in the dressing room. It may not have been the best break but he certainly had a good deal on the accommodation.

It was fitting that Bouchra, who had stood by her

husband throughout the entirety of the case, was outside the prison ready to pick her man up as he walked through the gates. It was like the triumphant scene at the end of a movie but van Persie would have come back to Earth with a bump when he was no doubt taken to task by Bouchra. The pair jetted out of the Netherlands and back to their London home, where they needed time to reflect on what had happened and how they would take things forward.

Elbali did not talk about what happened when the couple returned home, keeping it buttoned until May 2009 when the press agenda had moved on. She said he had certainly made a big mistake and that she was livid when she heard the news. Bouchra said she could have moved on and found another partner and probably would have done so if the pair hadn't been each other's first loves. Bouchra was different to many footballers' wives because she had not actively sought out a footballer as a husband.

Elbali's mother had advised against the relationship from its early days but had eventually come around to the idea. Mrs Elbali had protested that footballers were never serious when it came to relationships and she would be messed around. He was certainly a troubled character but also had a caring, honest side to his personality that shone through those more undesirable areas.

She told the *Sun*: 'It would have been easy at the time to leave him. I was a very angry girl. I could have continued with my life and found another guy. But I didn't want that because what we have together is very special. I don't think there's anybody else in the world who is like him. Every human being is allowed to make a mistake.

'It sounds strange to say it, but after that time we now

have an even better relationship. It has brought the best out of both of us. It was a break point – did we stop or did we continue? He was my first serious boyfriend and I was his first serious girlfriend. Every morning we get up together and Robin makes breakfast for all of us and then we have a shower together. He is so honest and lovely.'

With this incident van Persie became the latest in a string of Premier League players to be linked to rape. Cases were brought against several stars but none of them were convicted – with some people arguing girls had been making claims to get a slice of money and fame and others saying it was a reflection of the success of the highly-paid legal teams the players were able to afford.

In 2003 Leeds United midfielder Jody Morris and a friend were accused of raping a woman they had met in a bar – the charges were later dropped. A year later Leicester City players Paul Dickov, Frank Sinclair and Keith Gillespie were held for six days after being accused of rape at a Spanish training camp. The Leicester three were never convicted and van Persie joined this list of players who had proved they were falsely accused.

As footballers became more highly paid and increasingly well known from the 1990s onwards, the number of people leeching off them increased. Some girls aspired to become a 'WAG' – the term coined for wives and girlfriends of players. It had looked like van Persie had managed to escape this pitfall by marrying his childhood sweetheart but he fell foul of a wannabe WAG when he came across Sandra Boma Krijgsman.

He may not have been charged with rape but he had still cheated on his wife.

CHAPTER 4

BOUNCING BACK

Robin van Persie was determined to become more of a major player in the Arsenal team in the 2005/2006 season after what he had admitted had been an inconsistent previous season. He said a lot of young players could play an absolute blinder one game then be pretty quiet in the next and he wanted to put an end to this cycle. He was right to say this because it was one thing to put in a promising performance and another to be consistently brilliant and someone team mates would feel able to rely on.

He told the *Independent* he knew there would be plenty of chances to impress in English football: 'In England you have a lot of games and a lot of big games as well. For example, I didn't start the big, big games against Manchester United in the Premiership last season. But that's no problem, the boss has to choose the best team. That's not a strange decision.

'Every game I play I want to do something for the team

and do everything it takes to make a good impression. I am waiting for the boss and when he thinks Robin is really ready for it that's up to him. If he says that I am ready for the big games as well then I will be there.'

This was a timely message to Arsène Wenger – he was thankful the hellish summer break was over and pleased to be back in north London. Van Persie was clearly willing to wait his turn at Arsenal, showing great respect for his manager when he said he understood why he had been left out for certain games.

Wenger allowed him an extra week to recover from the ordeal as club doctors were concerned that the worry and stress of spending weeks in virtual isolation would have left van Persie worn out. The last thing they wanted was to rush him back and risk either fatigue or a possible flash point as there was now plenty of material for wind-up merchants to tease him with. It was an extremely sensible decision to leave van Persie out of that summer's Amsterdam pre-season tournament as the backlash would have been unbearable. It had been bad enough the year before when all he had done was leave Feyenoord, but now he had been accused and not yet cleared of raping a young woman, the Amsterdam Arena and surrounding areas would surely have been hell on earth.

His father agreed with the decision and said that things had got so bad when Robin was still playing in his homeland that a kick-boxer had had to be hired to provide protection. Bob said it was best to be careful because there were people in Amsterdam who wanted to kill his son. Unfortunately the artist had an important exhibition of his work on show at the time of his son's arrest; what was meant to be a time of celebration and recognition of his work was turned into a media circus as he was pursued by reporters.

Football is never worth risking life and limb for and at this controversial stage in his life, a trip to Amsterdam would surely have been too much for anybody to cope with. That 'raised on the streets' fighting talk had to be superseded by a concern for personal safety. It also had to be remembered that the tournament was a build-up for the whole team, not just van Persie, and if he were to travel with team mates the whole trip could have turned into a circus. Wenger would have been an angry man if Arsenal's preparations for an important season were interrupted.

It was a massive season for Arsenal as they needed to wrestle the Premier League trophy back from Chelsea and sought to progress further in the Champions League. Russian billionaire Roman Abramovich had taken over Arsenal's London rivals in 2003 and injected hundreds of millions of pounds into the club. Their 'special' manager José Mourinho led the team to the Premier League and League Cup in his first season at the helm and Arsenal would have to seriously up their game to match the big spenders.

Rather than ignoring the rivals and getting on with his own thing, Wenger moaned that Chelsea now dictated the transfer market and he would have to feed off the scraps the Blues left behind. Preparation for the campaign was made all that much harder by the departure of club captain Patrick Vieira to Juventus for just under £14 million. It seemed Arsenal were treading water in the transfer market while other clubs were getting better.

Van Persie missed the traditional mid-July pre-season trip

to neighbours Barnet but joined up with his team mates for their Austrian training camp. Those rape allegations were still hanging over his head and it must have been difficult to concentrate on his football with the threat of court proceedings still lingering.

With van Persie in Austria, a Rotterdam police spokeswoman said that the investigations were still ongoing and that it was impossible for the force to say when everything would be completed. Things would hopefully be resolved in August but with a backlog of cases to sort, it could be well into September until the issue was fully resolved.

Wenger hoped the situation would not drag on for too much longer because he knew this was not an easy thing for anybody to deal with. He said: 'I think it helps Robin to be with his comrades again. He has coped with it all quite well and I think being with his team mates every day can help him to forget about it a little bit. But it is never going to be easy for him.'

Hopefully being back with those team mates would instil a sense of normality in a life that had been thrown into chaos. A bit of a joke with team mates would be just what the doctor ordered after weeks of legal proceedings, prison cells and those likely showdown talks with Bouchra to try and save his marriage.

His great mentor Dennis Bergkamp would certainly have had a few choice words for his Dutch brother. Bergkamp had been a great help to van Persie at the time of his M25 car crash incident and would probably have provided him with some sound advice – probably something along the lines of 'keep your head down, son'.

As van Persie did his best to 'get on with it', Wenger

praised that mental strength that we had all heard about before but never had the chance to see in action. He reasoned that the trauma was too much to see him make an instant return to match action, especially in Amsterdam where he was a figure of hate at the best of times. Appearing in the Amsterdam Arena would have put too much psychological pressure on a player who was still understandably behind most of his team mates in the fitness stakes.

Wenger said: 'I have seen people go to jail for three days and come back destroyed. But he has come back good and showed a lot of strength, humility and desire to do well. It was a big trauma but he is recovering. I didn't want to put him under that psychological pressure and prefer to let him prepare. He has my full support. I believe he'll be a great, great player.'

That desire to do well on the football pitch was one of Wenger's main reasons for shelling out nearly £3 million on a player with a disruptive reputation. He was probably itching to kick a football during his time inside and the thought of getting back in an Arsenal shirt was most likely what got him through those two hellish weeks sat locked inside 'the greenhouse'.

As July drew to a close it looked like the rape charges might soon be dropped as an Arsenal club statement said they were confident the case would be closed within the next few days. The statement claimed the 'ordeal' would soon be over and reminded fans that van Persie had always maintained his innocence. The statement finished: 'His wife and the club stood by him because they knew he was innocent. Everyone at the club just hopes that he will be able to put it all behind him by the start of the new season.

He has a great strength of character and is slowly recovering from spending time in jail.'

The club clearly knew something the rest of the world didn't when they released a statement reassuring fans the sorry saga would soon be over. Sales of shirts with 'van Persie 11' on the back were probably not going so well. The source went on to say van Persie had been told he would not be charged over the allegations and would just have to wait for bits of paperwork to be completed before receiving official confirmation from the Rotterdam police.

In his extra time off, van Persie went for a break with Bouchra to the south of France to escape the unwanted attention. After getting somewhere near fitness, Robin van Persie was finally ready to pull on an Arsenal shirt again in the team's low-key friendly away to Belgian minnows Beveren.

After announcing van Persie would play a part in the game, Wenger said that the club had to accept that the player was still under investigation from the authorities but that he gave him total support and felt he was slowly getting over the incident. He certainly did play a part in the game as he led the line in the absence of Dennis Bergkamp and Thierry Henry. Not only did he complete the full 90 minutes without tiring but marked a happy return with two goals in an entertaining 3-3 draw. He scored twice in the last 20 minutes to seal an impressive return to action.

It must have been a thrill to experience the freedom of the football field again. He later said: 'I was so happy to play, to be outside, to smell the fresh air and make jokes with my team mates. I wasn't sad or anything. "Yes," I thought, "I'm free and ready to play football." I felt free again.'

Wenger must have been pleased with what he saw from the dugout and chirped after the game: 'This was his first game because he was given some extra holiday, but he has my full support. I think whatever problems you have in life, if you have another passion it can help you to cope because it gives you something else to focus on.

Arsène Wenger looked like a mastermind as he had handled the whole saga perfectly and eased the player back into action in a subdued friendly. But there came another mad twist in the erratic rollercoaster that was Robin van Persie's life – Marco van Basten called him up to the 30-man Netherlands squad for their high-profile match against Germany later that month. If that was not crazy enough, given what had happened recently and the fact that there was still the possibility of a court appearance on the horizon, the game would be played in Rotterdam.

Marco van Basten came under fire after naming the controversial figure in his squad. Van Persie was hardly a Dutch national hero as it was and some of the team's fans felt uneasy about someone with criminal proceedings hanging over his head representing their country. People who had been convicted for serious crimes have continued to play the game – West Bromwich Albion striker Lee Hughes was jailed in 2004 for causing death by dangerous driving but turned out for Oldham Athletic and Notts County following his 2007 release. Surely it was not too much of a problem for van Persie to pull on the orange shirt?

Van Basten said he only looked at the footballing skills of players and overlooked the charged levelled against van Persie. He argued that everybody deserved a second chance in life: 'We picked van Persie because he impressed as a player and as a person the last time he made the squad. I know he is still a suspect, but it is not my job to judge him. Even if he is convicted, I believe that everyone deserves a chance of rehabilitation.'

Just a few months after spending weeks behind bars in the notorious prison, van Persie was told he could be heading to one of the city's more attractive buildings – De Kuip. The good news just kept on coming as Wenger also said van Persie was in consideration for the squad to face Chelsea as Arsenal attempted to win the season-opening Charity Shield for a second year running.

Sadly Arsenal were no match for Chelsea's galaxy of stars and the Blues should have won by a much wider margin than the final score of 2-1. Didier Drogba was out to prove his worth to boss José Mourinho and he skipped past Philippe Senderos with less than 10 minutes gone to open the scoring. Despite all the pre-match talk, it was still something of a surprise when van Persie skipped on to the field at the start of the second half in place of Bergkamp. Drogba soon scored his second to effectively kill the game but, after Cesc Fàbregas had pulled one back for the Gunners, van Persie showed promising signs as he started to get involved in the game.

Alexander Hleb did well to win possession for the Reds and provide a half-chance for van Persie, who had to stretch to reach the pass and shot just wide of the target as it ran away from him. Chelsea were too much for Arsenal and van Persie was still a bit off the pace after having missed most of the pre-season action. No matter – a last-minute friendly at non-league side Boreham Wood proved just the tonic for van Persie as the Arsenal strikers found their shooting boots.

It was a battle between the two reserve strikers – Reyes and van Persie – to prove who was the better man. In a net-bothering eight-goal thriller, Reyes hit three to van Persie's two as Arsenal ran out 6-2 winners. Van Persie looked sharp as he was first on the scene after Reyes had a shot blocked and he made no mistake on the volley. A trademark curling shot doubled his tally and van Persie was only denied a hat-trick when goalkeeper Steve Corry parried away his free-kick – only for Robert Pires to tap home.

This season was to be Arsenal's last at the iconic Highbury stadium, with a move round the corner to a larger, more modern stadium on the cards. The club might have lost its captain in the close season but those younger players were beginning to mature nicely and the team would be looking to give a fitting send-off to the famous old ground.

They needed to get things off to a good start against Newcastle United on the opening day. Graeme Souness' men got their season off to a terrible start when Jermaine Jenas was red carded on the half-hour mark for a tackle on Gilberto Silva that looked like a wild kick from an angry horse. Arsenal lacked a certain conviction as they stroked the ball around beautifully but were guilty of not taking the chances they had created for themselves.

With time ticking away, Wenger brought on van Persie and his faith was rewarded as two late goals gave them victory at Highbury. Thierry Henry edged a penalty past the impressive Shay Given with 10 minutes left and van Persie was on hand to gleefully put the finishing touch to a wonderfully crafted Arsenal move with time almost up. This was the perfect way for him to silence critics and show that the whole rape case saga would not stand in the way of a talented young footballer. Hopefully this had put water under the bridge between the two.

Wenger was thrilled with the way van Persie had put that awful summer behind him with yet another starring role after coming off the bench, saying: 'His goal was important for his confidence and he was given a good reception by the fans. Van Persie can be a very important player. He has a sense for goals. He can finish inside or outside of the box.'

Wenger was still cautious with the case not yet completely closed and said he had been in dialogue with Netherlands coach van Basten so that the pair could manage the situation in the correct way. He said: 'I have spoken with Van Basten, who rates him really highly; he thinks he will become one of the big players in Holland. He is still not recovered. As long as this case is not concluded it will affect him.'

The Highbury boss spoke with caution and it was right that people did not get too carried away with his fantastic comeback if there was still the possibility that it could be cut short. Speculation that Wenger was looking to replace van Persie in the summer proved totally unfounded and he said van Persie was very much part of the club's future.

He said: 'I am optimistic and have complete faith in him and I don't believe for a second that we would lose him. He is working very hard, he has our support and we are all behind him. Let's pray it is over as quickly as possible.'

Marco van Basten was full of praise for the way Wenger had nurtured van Persie during his time in England. The fact that his national and club coaches communicated effectively with each other was of huge benefit to van Persie. It was common for club and international managers to clash, so this harmonious relationship under difficult circumstances was a breath of fresh air.

Van Basten said: 'Robin's development is absolutely amazing. I am really impressed by the way he is playing and training. I have never been so pleased with him. I have had very good talks with Arsène. We both believe in Robin and I have been pleased to find that Arsène and I are on the same wavelength when it comes to coaching, training and guiding Robin.

Bob van Persie had seen attempts to exhibit his artwork thwarted by a deluge of media attention and Robin had had his fair share of hassle from reporters too. The father figure had earned a reputation as a fine, unique artist who created crowd scenes from old newspapers and magazines.

His national coach revealed it was part of the deal that, if he was to pick the Arsenal man, he would not have to attend media interview sessions or television interviews alongside the other Netherlands players. Van Basten understood completely and said he could take as long a break from interaction with the media as he wanted.

As he said when the initial announcement was made, van Basten was only interested in how van Persie performed on the pitch: 'I am only interested in his performance as a player. He's had a lot to cope with this summer and he's handling it all very well. I know the media are on his back but everyone forgets that the police have never made an official accusation. So I feel for him and I will help him – just like they do at his club.'

With less sympathetic managers, he would surely not

have come so far so quickly after the summer, if at all. The tag team of Wenger and van Basten had worked wonders to get their man back to something like his best. The 22-year-old was all too aware of the leg-up the coaches had given him and he told them he appreciated the effort they had put in when others might have turned their back. Marco van Basten had allowed van Persie to duck out of the media spotlight when representing his country and he said he was happy with the protection the former Ajax and AC Milan striker had provided.

Although things weren't exactly perfect at the moment, van Persie was concentrating on football and trying to continue his life as normally as possible. Having a never-ending procession of high-profile games to take part in would certainly help take his mind off the troubles. He said: 'I wanted to have a nice holiday but it didn't turn out the way I expected. I have a problem but I'm concentrating on my football at the moment. I never thought about staying in England and not playing for the Dutch team. I have a goal and I can only reach that goal if I play in the Dutch team. I am happy with the way my football is going now.'

Chelsea again looked in a different class to Arsenal when the two sides met at Stamford Bridge. Freddie Ljungberg took a knock midway through the first half and van Persie came on to try and pose a more direct attacking threat. He flicked a volley wide of the goal, but money talks and Didier Drogba's goal gave Chelsea their first league win over the Gunners for 10 years.

There was some good news coming from Rotterdam after it was found that Sandra Boma Krijgsman had lied to police. Leaked reports revealed that when she called the emergency services she told operators she had been kidnapped so that officers would appear at the scene quicker. Hotel staff were apparently shocked the allegations had been made as she had sat downstairs in the bar for hours afterwards making relaxed telephone calls to friends.

She told police she had thought van Persie was a 'nice' man and wanted to have sex with him, but did not want to have sex with his two friends as well.

One statement Krijgsman made to police read: 'I really would have wanted to sleep with him if it had all passed off peacefully. But all three wanted sex with me, which wasn't really in my plans.'

The fact that her story was changing and she said she wanted to have sex with van Persie would surely have put certain question marks over her story. The case may have been rumbling on but the chance of it ever coming to trial were surely moving further and further away.

Crowd trouble before the game overshadowed the Netherlands' entertaining 2-2 friendly draw with Germany. Arjen Robben scored twice as van Persie played but hardly impressed – he looked a tired man and the occasion might have slightly got the better of him.

Things weren't much better when the Dutch faced a trip to Armenia in their World Cup qualifying group and van Persie was picked to start the game. Played out on the left wing, van Persie hardly put in a vintage display and van Basten substituted him during the underwhelming 1-0 win. He would need to be able to perform well in a number of positions in order to be a success story for his country as there was a lot of competition for places – especially in a country as blessed with attacking talent as the Netherlands.

Van Persie was honest enough to tell reporters he was not at his best in the game. He said: 'I wasn't pleased with my performance against Armenia. I tried to do things simply and when I tried something special I failed. It is important to be honest, positively or negatively, but I have a good contact with the trainer and I feel at ease in the team.'

In the game at home to Andorra just four days later, van Persie spurned a couple of good early chances as his disappointing form for the national side continued. Ruud van Nistelrooy and Rafael van der Vaart kindly showed him how it was done as the side strolled to a 4-0 win without breaking a sweat.

That good start was fading fast under the lights as a sublime flicked assist from van Persie could do nothing to stop his side slipping to a 2-1 reverse at Middlesbrough. This was certainly not title-winning form and van Persie had not been playing brilliantly since the opening day win over Newcastle.

The controversy surrounding the players reared its ugly head once again as Arsenal started their Champions League campaign by playing Swiss minnows FC Thun at fortress Highbury. There was a storm in a teacup in the build-up to the game when defender Emmanuel Eboué put in a strong tackle in a training exercise and hurt van Persie's shin and knee. The Ivory Coast player's unreserved apology was waved away by van Persie, who was extremely angry and later had the injury bandaged by medical staff.

Wenger moved quickly to deny a rift between the pair and cleared the Dutchman to play in the game. He was sorely needed because Thierry Henry would be missing for around six weeks with a groin strain.

Things had gone slightly pear-shaped on the training

pitch and they didn't exactly go to plan at Highbury either as Arsenal left it late to sneak a 2-1 victory against their Swiss opponents. On the stroke of half-time van Persie was chasing an inaccurate through ball and as he stretched to control the ball with his right foot raised up high, his studs clattered into the face of Alen Orman. It was completely accidental as his eyes were fixed on the incoming ball the entire time, and as the two players hit the deck, van Persie held up his hands to apologise. Polish referee Grzegorz Gilewski did not look at all impressed and a swarm of Thun players gathered to make the incident look like more of a flash point than it really was or needed to be.

Gilewski looked ready to combust as he gestured for the Thun medical team to come onto the field and raised his eyebrows as he forcefully blew his whistle. It looked like the referee's eyeballs were going to pop out of their sockets before he flashed the red card to draw gasps of disbelief from the Highbury crowd. In a final humiliation, the Pole then saw fit to push van Persie towards the tunnel as if he did not know where it was. In his younger years van Persie would have reacted angrily to this needless gesture from the man who had just sent him off but instead the 22-year-old simply trudged off the field without causing any further bother.

This red card was extremely unfortunate but it was the sort of luck that had followed van Persie around in recent years. There was no malicious intent but it was a correct decision by the referee because his boot caught Orman horribly. Had the roles been reversed, there would have been uproar in the North London stands. It was a great shame as he had started well and worried the goalkeeper with a couple of decent efforts. The incident was entirely unfortunate but van Persie had bounced back from far worse than this in recent years.

Dennis Bergkamp looked like a goody two-shoes when he prodded home Arsenal's last-minute winner as his countryman looked on enviously from the stands. Van Persie would learn from incidents like this and so although it was a short-term setback, in the long term this red card would be a lesson that he would learn from.

Arsène Wenger had a reputation to keep up and true to form he slated the referee in the post-match press conference, saying van Persie had been culpable of dangerous play but not violence. He said the sending off came as a complete surprise and was the wrong decision. Wenger fumed: 'It was not Robin's fault. It was an accident. Was van Persie very high? No. The referee was flying high. Maybe he wasn't watching the game.'

Unsurprisingly the Thun players were not too happy about the tackle – Arsenal would not have been either. Their notoriously straight-talking Australian defender Ljubo Milicevic had some strong words and a hilarious comparison to make after the game. He said: 'It was pretty brutal. Obviously van Persie didn't see the boy but what was he doing with a kung fu kick like that? It was very dangerous. I don't know how it looked on camera, but Bruce Lee would have been proud of it.' Orman agreed by saying that there was a time and a place for kick-boxing but the football field was not it.

Wenger would defend his players to the death but on this occasion he was simply wrong as that left boot had indeed been dangerously high when it clattered into the defender. It may not have been intentional from van Persie but it was still his boot that had done the damage and Orman left the game with six stitches and a severely bruised eye for his troubles. In return van Persie would be suspended for the mouth-watering trip to Amsterdam to face Ajax.

Things went a bit smoother when Arsenal got back into the swing of Premier League matters to beat Everton 2-0 at Highbury. Reyes set up van Persie cleverly and he was incredibly unlucky to see his volley hit the woodwork and bounce clear after a clever cushion and left-footed volley. After again going close and stinging the hands of veteran goalkeeper Nigel Martyn, he was lucky to escape injury after a nasty lunge from Phil Neville that quite rightly drew a yellow card from referee Alan Wiley.

With Henry still missing, van Persie did not do too much to stake his claim for a regular place in the side by again failing to score as the Gunners were held to a goalless draw at West Ham. Northern Ireland goalkeeper Roy Carroll was equal to his first-half effort and was also in the right place at the right time to block van Persie's wickedly deflected shot in the second half.

Finally van Persie found the back of the net – with the help of a deflection – to guide his side to a fine 1-0 home win over Birmingham City. After coming off the bench, his somewhat speculative effort clipped the leg of Stephen Clemence to wrong-foot goalkeeper Maik Taylor. Arsenal had looked out of ideas as the inspired Taylor repelled everything they threw at him, but van Persie shone after his introduction.

Wenger saluted his goal hero after the game: 'He is top class, has a good eye and a terrific shot. When he takes a shot in training the keeper has no chance. Today I was happy to score a scrappy goal. Van Persie gives you hope when he comes on.'

This was exactly the right time for van Persie to hit a rich vein of form as his team was desperately short up-front and his goals would be vital to the team's success. Wenger had been happy with the way his young star had been treated by the Netherlands coaching staff but would surely be less impressed when van Persie picked up a knock whilst training ahead of international duty. As the Dutch prepared for a World Cup Qualifiers showdown with rivals Czech Republic, van Persie hurt his leg when he collided with Hedwiges Maduro.

Van Persie was not fit enough to start the match but he was given a 10-minute run out at the end of the match. The damage had already been done by then as the Dutch sealed their place at the 2006 World Cup finals with a 2-0 win in Prague.

He started the match at home to Macedonia four days later but with qualification already sealed, the Dutch took their foot off the gas and played out an uninspiring 0-0 draw. Van Persie went close in Amsterdam but dragged his shot just wide of the goal and later admitted that it didn't quite happen for his team that night.

That niggling thigh strain would rule van Persie out of Arsenal's disastrous trip to The Hawthorns, where West Brom were waiting to ambush an injury-depleted side with a 2-1 win. Wenger virtually threw in the towel in the title race as he admitted it did not look like Arsenal could make up the points difference between themselves and the top of the table.

Somewhat predictably, he blamed the recent international

games for his team's injury crisis and subsequent Hawthorns failure. It was a poor excuse to use because all teams faced the same problem as Arsenal but not many other managers tried to fashion an excuse out of this.

If there was nothing for them in the Premier League this season, Arsenal could at least turn their attentions to mounting a serious challenge for one of the cups. Van Persie and Thierry Henry were both back to earn a starting place as their side travelled to Sparta Prague. The Dutchman had little to offer beyond a crunching tackle that was rewarded with a yellow card and his deliveries seemed a bit off-cue. Henry's two goals in a 2-0 win saw him overtake Ian Wright as Arsenal's all-time top goalscorer.

Van Persie scored a brace as a team of Wenger's kids impressed in a 3-0 League Cup win at Sunderland. After Eboué had opened the scoring on the hour mark, it was van Persie's time to shine. The striker evoked memories of that FA Cup final shoot-out win when he slammed a penalty into the top corner after Arturo Lupoli had been tripped in the box. As the game drew to a close, Seb Larsson slipped van Persie through and he nipped through a forest of tired Sunderland legs before slipping the ball past the advancing goalkeeper.

It was a brilliant night's work for van Persie and he was back to his best according to Wenger. Straight-talking Sunderland manager Mick McCarthy said that he had not been aware van Persie was 'as good as that' and when asked about the final goal which was carefully stroked home with a side-foot, he labelled the finish outstanding.

Although he was still only deemed worthy of a place on the bench for the league trip to bitter rivals Tottenham, van

Persie played a big part in a spirited comeback. Spurs led through Ledley King's deserved first-half opener when van Persie was brought on midway through the second period. The introduction of van Persie breathed new life into the visitors and immediately forced a good save from Paul Robinson. After another van Persie effort flashed tantalisingly along the goal-line, Robert Pires grabbed a point for Arsenal when he pounced on a weak downward punch from Robinson.

Tottenham's Dutch manager Martin Jol was full of praise for his countryman after the game: 'Van Persie has a marvellous touch, like Arjen Robben. We got a coach in a couple of weeks ago from Holland and he did an exercise with him for years. He was here today and I said to him "Hopefully you didn't teach him all the tricks." I was a bit worried about him because he looked eager to score. Van Persie is probably one of the players with the best first touch – in Holland, certainly.'

He was obviously doing something right because van Persie had earned glowing praise from opposition managers in consecutive games. Wenger was understandably pleased with the way his super sub had got in amongst the Spurs defenders after feeling his team was too stand-offish in the first half. After learning to play in the rough and tumble culture of street football, van Persie was not one to shy away from a challenge and would not leave any stone unturned in his quest to win back possession. If he had been back on the Kralingen streets, he would have desperately chased down the ball for fear of his team being ousted from the pitch.

Thierry Henry put the side on course to top their Champions League group when he put them ahead against

Sparta Prague at the start of November. It was a stunning goal from the Frenchman and he received a standing ovation from the Highbury crowd as van Persie was brought on in his place with half an hour remaining. After a couple of early range-finders didn't quite work out, van Persie turned predator to gobble up two half-chances.

With 10 minutes left Dennis Bergkamp fed the ball to Arsenal's form man who skipped around a couple of tackles to bury home from 20 yards out and make the game safe. Van Persie was often praised for possessing an excellent first touch but he later told reporters his initial touch had been 'a bit poor' and that had forced him to jink around the Sparta defenders before working the ball onto his left foot and spanking home.

Van Persie turned on the style to make it two goals in five minutes when he slotted Eboué's cross home. The ball came in hard and low but the Dutchman instinctively stuck out his right boot and the ball was in the back of the net once more.

Arsenal might have trailed moneybags Chelsea by 14 points but van Persie said that after qualifying for the last 16 of the Champions League, Arsenal now had to try their best to claw back some of the ground that the Blues had opened up. He said: 'We are through in the Champions League and now we have to fight for the Premiership. It is a dream for me to win that one day and I think it is possible. Everybody says Chelsea this and Chelsea that. Okay, they have a good squad – but we have a good squad as well and we are fighting for the Premiership title. At the end we will see where we will finish.'

After shyly batting away another comparison to Dennis Bergkamp, van Persie denied speculation he was becoming frustrated at a lack of starts despite racking up the goals in his substitute appearances. He said it was completely up to Wenger and he was happy with whatever opportunity was given to him to play. The respect between player and manager had been evident for a while and van Persie enthused that Wenger had been a fantastic figure in his life since moving to England. It was clear that a steady father figure was what van Persie needed to settle him down and, with Bob working on his artwork across the sea, the Frenchman would have to make do for now.

He was also quick to heap praise on the Highbury stars who had inspired him to become a better player. Sol Campbell, Henry and Bergkamp had set the perfect example for any young players by playing with spirit and always trying their best, whether during matches or in training.

Bergkamp said it was natural that the previous season had been one of transition for van Persie and that this term would be when he would show his true worth: 'When you start at a new club with a new team, you expect to have to deal with things that you don't get straight away. We helped him with that because it is something we have been through. The good thing is that he listens and he has a lot of respect. That is the first thing you have to do – and he can only get better.'

That respect had been difficult for some to understand but it had been present throughout van Persie's stint at Arsenal. He did not back-chat coaches as had happened at Excelsior and Feyenoord, and he listened to the advice of old heads like Bergkamp, whereas as a youngster at Feyenoord he had crossed swords with legendary striker Pierre van Hooijdonk.

Bergkamp commended van Persie's resilience in the face of his problems that summer. He said hitting the back of the net was the most important thing for any striker: 'A lot of things have come his way on and off the pitch but if you see him playing football after these moments, he is still the same. He has a lot of confidence. It looks like arrogance but we know it is confidence. He can score and that is the most important thing in football. He is confident, getting stronger and he has skill. It looks fantastic for the future.'

But when statisticians revealed that van Persie averaged a goal every 1.5 games, a rate better than Thierry Henry's goal every 1.6 games, Bergkamp suggested that things were easier for a player coming off the bench like van Persie had been doing. Bergkamp said that the pace of the game can drop late in games and if somebody comes on with a fresh pair of legs, they are at a distinct advantage.

That string of super sub appearances was finally rewarded with a starting place as Arsenal comfortably saw off relegation candidates Sunderland 3-1 at Highbury. It only took van Persie 12 minutes to make an impact as he slotted home after latching onto a well-measured Sol Campbell through ball. Van Persie was clearly out to make the most of being given a starting berth and expertly chested the ball down and unleashed a left-footed drive that beat 18-year-old goalkeeper Ben Alnwick at his near post.

His pace was unmatchable and it could have been so many more for an attacking Arsenal side as Henry scored two – one as a result of a gorgeous van Persie flick – and Reyes was also a threat. With the scores tied, Alnwick was beaten all ends up by a wonderfully aware right-footed van Persie lob that only just went wide of the goal, and the

Dutchman went even closer later on when he brilliantly controlled and shot on the turn only to see his effort crash off the woodwork.

Bergkamp said it was harder to play matches from the start but van Persie now had an impressive record of six goals in six starts. After the duo had starred together – combining well to carve out goalscoring opportunities – Wenger said there was good potential for the two to work together in the future because they were both more than capable of finding the back of the net.

Wenger said: 'At the moment, I feel that he's the closest prospect to partner Thierry Henry as a central striker. He doesn't have the experience and the final ball of Dennis Bergkamp but he can score goals and has some class as well.'

Bergkamp was an invaluable tool when it came to learning the tricks of the trade but it would be Henry whom van Persie was more likely to play alongside in the future. The great motivator and lover of mind games Wenger dangled a massive carrot in front of the 22-year-old when he said van Persie had the ingredients to be as good as Bergkamp but that 'the biggest part is to do it'. He had been given a clear message to 'grow up or else' and it was obviously this kind of strong message that the wayward wonder-kid had needed all along.

The next person to be asked the tiresome question about the similarities between Bergkamp and van Persie was Thierry Henry. The Frenchman said it was not possible to create another Dennis Bergkamp and van Persie was his own man. He reasoned that whilst van Persie loved to dribble his way past as many players as possible, Bergkamp was different because his 'super power' was to kill a defence with one incredible pass.

He said when somebody had the brilliant attitude of van Persie, nobody was able to stop them. Henry said: 'Robin is really confident. Without going too far he has everything a footballer would dream to have. Robin can play anywhere he wants. I am not joking, it is up to him and his desire. I think the goals he scored away at Sunderland in the League Cup gave him a lot of confidence. One thing I like about him at the moment is that he wants to go and score.

'That is the most important thing for a striker. He just wants to go behind the defence and get into the box. The first goal at home to Sunderland was amazing. Sol put in an incredible ball with his left foot and Robin made a run behind their defence. He has done that a lot and it is a sign he just wants to put the ball in the back of the net.'

Putting the ball in the back of the net was the thing that really counted and van Persie had been doing a lot of that in recent weeks following a poor start to the season. Henry appreciated having a hungry young man playing alongside him who was ready and willing to run through and beyond the opposition back line.

With the van Persie love-in taking place after yet another star performance, Wenger became twitchy about what would happen in the future. Like a young man popping the question after being worried other blokes were eyeing up his girlfriend, Wenger announced he wanted to sign the striker under an even longer-term contract than the four-year deal he signed back in 2004. What had emerged from Henry and Bergkamp's praise was that far from being 'the next so and so', van Persie was very much his own man and a unique talent. He was in arguably the form of his life and had the potential to catapult Arsenal towards success in one of the cup competitions that season.

All strikers have a secret goal target they want to get from a season and van Persie said that with his side in contention for four competitions, he had the opportunity to push for a lot of goals. He said: 'We're still in all four competitions so I think a minimum 15-20 isn't an unrealistic target. Hopefully it's more, as my record so far is 23. I have got six already. I know I'm still improving and with hard work and the managers supporting me, then I can only get better.'

Incredibly van Persie was at it again when Arsenal edged to a 3-2 victory at Wigan Athletic. Once again given the opportunity to start a match by Wenger, van Persie again delivered the goods for his team. In just the 11th minute he cracked a 25-yard left-footed shot through the arms of goalkeeper John Filan. Once again it was a Sol Campbell punt that he latched onto before sneaking past countryman Arjan de Zeeuw and beating Filan for the first time in over eight hours. Henry again starred as he hit two goals to remind supporters that he was the club's number one striker.

Van Persie's performance surprised Wigan, according to their midfielder Graham Kavanagh. He said: 'I really didn't think Robin van Persie was anywhere near as good as he is. He scored one fantastic goal and was instrumental in everything they did. He was a problem all afternoon because he has a wonderful left foot, so much pace and so many tricks. Arsenal have rested players but when you have a player like van Persie on the pitch it is very little consolation.'

There was speculation that Henry might move away from Highbury in the summer and Wenger was doing everything he could to tie his countryman down to the side. The manager said Henry's partnership with van Persie was brilliant and might become something truly special if only they had the chance to spend more time playing together.

Wenger said: 'Henry and van Persie – I don't know if there's a better partnership but they are developing well. We know all about Thierry. But it's good that Robin scores, develops, shows strength. There are signs he can take over the mantle from Dennis Bergkamp, though we have to give it time.'

Bergkamp and the younger Dutchman were always mentioned in the same sentence and that was something that would probably never stop happening. Van Persie played in a similar position to the elder statesman, even if the way he contributed to the team was different, and so with Bergkamp coming towards the end of his Arsenal career and van Persie at the start of his, it was natural for there to be talk of their switchover.

He was not much of a talker traditionally, but Bergkamp began to open up as his career drew to a conclusion. He pointed out that the two were very different because van Persie loved to have the ball at his feet and take it to defenders whilst Bergkamp preferred running on to a pass. Bergkamp agreed that the two were similar in that they both created chances and, most importantly of all, scored goals.

Van Persie had mind games to contend with ahead of Arsenal's trip to FC Thun, where he would come up against Alen Orman, the man he'd pole-axed in the sides' meeting at Highbury two months previously. Orman must have thought he was being clever when he said: 'I'm okay with it as you sometimes expect these things in football but I don't know what our fans will do to him.'

Van Persie had dealt with hostile environments at White Hart Lane and the Amsterdam Arena and this threat ahead of the visit to Stade de Suisse would hardly have had the worrying effect Orman might have wished for. Ten minutes before the break van Persie was again involved in a red card incident but this time the foul had been committed against him. As he galloped towards goal after being released by Freddie Ljungberg, centre back Armand Deumi pulled him down. The foul was outside the box but the Cameroon defender was sent off and van Persie nearly made his team pay instantly when he flashed the resulting free-kick just over the crossbar.

Roughhousing tactics would not stop Arsenal from playing decent football and van Persie nearly broke the deadlock after excellent combination play with Reyes. Orman had promised van Persie a tough time but surely if this rough treatment created goalscoring opportunities for his team, van Persie would not have been overly concerned. With the game plodding along to a goalless conclusion, Selver Hodži continued this 'rough treatment' of van Persie by bringing him down in the penalty area to give the Gunners a spot-kick that could nick all three points and see them top the group. Robert Pires converted and the Gunners had topped their group after winning all their games to go through as seeds in the draw.

He had taken a lot of knocks in the game but, unlike last season, he was able to pick himself up from them and get on with the game. Van Persie had definitely bulked himself up to deal with the rough and tumble of life in the Premier League and it looked like this step was also paying dividends in the Champions League.

Wenger said muscle powder had been the order of the day: 'Physically he looks stronger – last year he looked a bit weak to adapt to the English game. Then in the second part of last season he started to score some goals and show more presence. He looked a bit lean and weak when he came to us and we have had to strengthen him. He is much stronger now and resists the challenges that he didn't before.'

When Blackburn visited Highbury for another comfortable 3-0 defeat, Wenger left van Persie on the bench because he did not want to 'over play' the 22-year-old, who apparently needed to become a more consistent performer. After Cesc Fàbregas opened the scoring, Thierry Henry scored his 100th league goal at Highbury – a club record and, with the stadium in its last season of use, one that would never be beaten. Van Persie joined the party late on and did his best to steal the limelight from Henry with an incredible goal.

After receiving the ball with his back to goal, van Persie twisted and turned and headed out to the right-hand touchline. It looked like there was no route to goal but quick as a flash van Persie darted towards goal and somehow slipped his way in between Michael Gray and Robbie Savage as if they were not there at all. As he approached the penalty area the Dutchman unleashed an unstoppable shot that the legendary George Best, who had recently passed away and received a minute's applause from supporters and players before kick-off, would surely have been proud of.

The crowd went ballistic and van Persie went over to embrace supporters on the far side of the ground after scoring what he said was his best goal so far for Arsenal. He had done brilliantly just to keep the ball on the pitch but the left-footed sweep that followed his mazy run was something else because Brad Friedel was an imposing figure in the Blackburn goal and to beat him took some doing. It was just the latest in a long line of awesome strikes and van Persie certainly had an eye for the spectacular. Sometimes he had been accused of being selfish and ignoring players in better positions but when you had the skills to go it alone, as van Persie did, it must have been very tempting to try to beat teams on his own.

Despite notching some memorable strikes, van Persie was still not a regular starter under Wenger. The Dutch super-sub insisted he was happy with Wenger's squad rotation policy. He joked that Wenger had likened him to a cobra because he knew the benefits of lying in wait to ambush the opposition after being released from Arsenal's wicker basket. He showed great modesty when he said that although it was great to have scored so many goals in the last few games, this was what the club was paying his wages for in the first place.

This was van Persie's seventh goal in as many games and Thierry Henry said the audacity of his shot showed the Dutchman was clearly a man with confidence in his own abilities: 'He was at a difficult angle and he still took his chance and scored. That's when a striker is playing at the peak of his confidence.'

Van Persie noted that Arsenal should only be judged by where they ended up in the league at the end of the season:

'We made a slow start, but the season is like a marathon and the only thing that counts is where we are at the end. I've got great hope for the rest of the season. I accepted not starting. I played in the previous two games so I just get on with it. I'm still young and the boss plays me quite a lot, so I don't have any reason to complain.

'I have to play well and score or make assists. In the past seven games I've been happy with that. If you come on in the last 15 or 20 minutes you can be very effective. I will do everything to continue this if the boss gives me the chance, and I feel I've taken a step forward.'

It was clear van Persie was very happy with the way things were going for him and did not mind not starting every match as long as the goals kept on coming. He had been assigned the super-sub role and did not mind coming on in different positions so long as he was on the field and involved in the game at one stage or another. It showed great maturity and self-belief that he was not in the manager's face demanding a guaranteed starting place as some young stars might have done. Wayne Rooney for one would have been having none of it and would probably have had a transfer request on the manager's desk first thing in the morning.

With December fast approaching, there was still a possibility of a charge being made over those rape allegations. Wenger praised the way his man had continued his career and said the club was hopeful the matter would draw to a close sooner rather than later. He said: 'Everybody would have been affected by what happened to him. He was in jail for two weeks and from one day to the next there were a lot of questions around him. So it is difficult to take, especially if you feel you have done nothing wrong. I feel he has got over it and the signs are looking good.'

Van Persie made it eight goals in eight games with yet another strike as Wenger's kids comfortably saw off Reading 3-0 in the League Cup. It seemed everything he touched was turning into goals and he shone brightly in this win. He went close early on with a well-struck effort that was goal-bound but cannoned off a defender's legs.

After intelligently spreading play to the wing, van Persie darted for the penalty area and Reyes deftly touched the ball into his path; the Dutchman rifled a left-footed shot into the bottom corner past the dive of former Arsenal stopper Graham Stack. He ran away kissing the club crest on his shirt and the junior Gunners – with an average age of just 19 – huddled together to celebrate. It was a brilliant united picture and perfectly encapsulated that team spirit that Wenger and van Persie liked to bang on about.

As his goalscoring run continued, Wenger remarked that every time van Persie touched the ball it looked as though something special was going to happen. He claimed that Reyes, who also put one past Stack, and van Persie were two special young players who would go on to have excellent futures in the game. Surely it would soon be time for van Persie to be given more of a chance in the first team and leave the 'B Team' League Cup games in the past to allow some of the club's emerging talent more of a chance to prove themselves without van Persie there to steal their thunder?

Once again the Gunners boss put that goalscoring run down to the hunger van Persie had shown after being released from that June jail cell hell: 'When you experience being adored at the age of 20, and then you're confined for two weeks with a lot of negative publicity, it was certainly a shock for him. It took him some time to recover from that. I worried for him.' It took real guts to bounce back from something as dramatic and upsetting as that summer had been for van Persie. It was most fortunate that he was a big personality in a situation that would have seen less strong-willed players wilt under the pressure.

With his season going so well and Bergkamp on the way out, it was put to van Persie that he could take on the club's number 10 shirt in the 2006/07 season. At any club it was a hallowed shirt but at Arsenal it had become synonymous with Bergkamp after he held down the shirt for over a decade. Van Persie said he would refuse to wear the number 10 shirt because he had too much respect for what Bergkamp had done and he wanted to do things his own way. After being hailed left, right and centre as the elder statesman's replacement, he was determined to retain his independence and be recognised as a great player in his own right.

The respect van Persie had for Bergkamp was absolute. He continued to refuse to be compared to Bergkamp, who had given the club an amazing 10 years of service. He told the *Sunday Mirror* he had learned so much from the enigma and he knew how privileged he was to have mixed with Bergkamp.

He said: 'Dennis was a giant. I have only just arrived on the big scene and I still have a lot to prove. Ask me the same question in 10 years' time. At this moment I would not dare compare myself with Dennis Bergkamp. When you're a young, talented player you can't wish for anybody better in your team than Dennis. I can only speak highly about him.

At Arsenal he was always there for me. I feel so privileged that I was allowed to train and play with him for two years.'

Things were ticking along nicely for the Gunners and it was only right that van Persie was rewarded for his performances with the Premier League 'Player of the Month' award for November. When called by the Arsenal press office with news of the award, van Persie said 'OK very funny, who's really won it?' A few years back he would have had some kind of smart response but now he had been carefully matured in Wenger's cask, van Persie had become an award-winning mellow whisky. Van Persie was a more humble man than he used to be and was genuinely surprised by the recognition his performances had received. Perhaps he had become so used to ignoring negative publicity that he had stopped listening to the media altogether and that was why he was shocked at the award. Maybe praise from the likes of Mick McCarthy and Martin Jol had passed him by.

The 'Player of the Month' and 'Manager of the Month' awards were always said to be cursed by fans because as soon as they received the recognition their hard work deserved, things tended to go pear-shaped. That poisoned chalice looked to have affected van Persie as he did not look up to scratch in a 2-0 defeat at Bolton Wanderers. In an awful start to December, van Persie and his team would go on to draw a blank in four consecutive matches.

Van Persie sliced wide of the Bolton goal in a frustrating afternoon at the Reebok Stadium. It looked like the striker had got the Gunners back in the game but after he rippled the netting, the linesman's flag was raised and referee Howard Webb blew for a free-kick after Thierry Henry was ruled to have fouled Tal Ben Haim in the build-up. It had been one of those days for van Persie because when he had finally done something right, a team mate had let him down.

Arsenal looked a million miles away from the title contenders they had said they were at the start of the season. Another game against his old rivals Ajax was not really what van Persie needed right now but with the team already confirmed as winners of their Champions League qualifying group, there was nothing riding on the game. After Henry missed a penalty, van Persie nearly nicked a win at the death when a mazy run and curling shot cannoned off the outstretched boot of the lucky goalkeeper Maarten Stekelenburg.

At the start of December Arsenal unfurled the bunting to announce that van Persie was all set to sign an extended contract and stay at the club until 2011. This deal was van Persie's reward for finally adapting to the Arsenal method of playing – less individual skill and showboating, more slick, swift passing and awareness of team mates. Arsène Wenger confirmed that van Persie had earned a longer stay at Arsenal after progressing from individual talent to team player.

He said: 'Robin will sign in the coming days. He's come on a lot. He was tempted to use his talent in an individual way but has developed into a team player and will be a big player if he continues to do that.'

Wenger had been eyeing up Michael Owen as a summer signing – the former Liverpool striker had burst onto the scene for club and country in his teenage years like van Persie but things had turned stale after a big-money move to Real Madrid. Wenger eventually decided against a move he said would go against the philosophy of the side he had built.

He said: 'I was tempted by Owen but it was a question of "Do I stick to what I started or take a completely different direction?" I hoped Van Persie and José Reyes would give us goals and I had to bring my young players in at some stage.'

Luckily for van Persie the ship was sailing in a straight line with Wenger at the helm. Some were scornful of his policy of fielding sides packed with youngsters for League Cup games, but Wenger's production line of talent was progressing nicely and the likes of Reyes and van Persie were at the forefront of this new movement.

Van Persie was understandably thrilled at the prospect of committing his long-term future to Arsenal. It must have come as a great relief that Wenger did not have his head turned and had complete faith in his potential to be a brilliant player. The club had taken in the robin with a broken wing, nursed it back to health and watched with joy as it began to fly better than ever before. Football was the most important thing in his life and with his future at the club secure for many years he would be free to concentrate on playing and nothing else.

He chirped: 'I'm extremely pleased with life here. Arsenal are a formidable club and with my new contract, I don't have to worry about anything other than football. This is exactly what I want – to focus on training and playing games to become an even better player.'

The contract would keep him at the club for six years and van Persie was delighted to be tied down for so long because he wanted to pay back Wenger and the club for the faith showed in him. The new deal also proved a tidy little earner as it was rumoured to more than double van Persie's weekly wage packet to £35,000 a week. Not bad for a player who was not even usually on the field for the full 90 minutes.

Just before Christmas it looked like Chelsea had killed off Arsenal's title challenge as they grabbed a controversial 2-0 win at Highbury. Once again van Persie had a goal ruled out for offside – luck had well and truly deserted him since receiving that wretched 'Player of the Month' award. There was nothing wrong at all with van Persie's wonderfully taken goal and he was understandably aghast at the decision.

He had stolen possession and marched forward and expertly turned his man before rolling the ball past Petr Cech. Thierry Henry had been in an offside position but was not interfering with play so the goal should have been allowed to stand. Wenger was predictably livid and was at the edge of his technical area voicing his displeasure and van Persie was booked for dissent in the aftermath. Michael Essien heaped on the misery with a clattering challenge on van Persie that saw him lucky to escape with a yellow card.

Chelsea boss José Mourinho had managed to get under the skin of Wenger and he was still fuming after the final whistle. He came out to ask why van Persie's goal had been ruled out but the protest bordered on the ridiculous and would later see him in hot water with the FA. His rant smacked of sour grapes when he accused the match officials of being part of the Chelsea team. Wenger moaned: 'It was the linesman who flagged, but I see the referee and the linesmen as part of the same team. . . the Chelsea team.'

This defeat had understandably dealt a body blow to Arsenal as both van Persie and Wenger allowed their frustrations to boil over. Keith Hackett, the man in charge of the Professional Game Match Officials Board – the governing body for referees – later said van Persie's goal should have stood.

A couple of days after the game, Hackett said: 'Arsenal have talked to me and questioned the offside decision. I was able to confirm it was not a correct decision by the assistant referee. The assistant puts his flag up in the belief Henry becomes active – but, when you examine the video many times, you can see he's not active.'

This came too little too late for Arsenal and would have only rubbed salt into the wounds of that crushing defeat. And when Arsenal were only just able to scrape past Doncaster Rovers in a League Cup penalty shoot-out, van Persie had real wounds to lick. The uncompromising Steve Roberts left the Dutchman writhing in agony with a crunching tackle that left van Persie needing treatment to his left knee. He had to be withdrawn just minutes later after being reduced to hobbling around the pitch.

As the season entered the notoriously busy Christmas period, van Persie was receiving more knocks than a front door. He had boasted of mental strength but was van Persie's body made of the same stuff? As he was ruled out for a few games, it looked like it wasn't. At the turn of the year van Persie was still struggling with that ankle injury and put in an uneventful appearance in a 0-0 bore draw at Villa Park. He was well off 100 per cent but re-joined the side as they hosted feisty Cardiff City at Highbury.

Glenn Loovens was on loan to the Welsh side from Feyenoord but it would not be a happy reunion for the former team mates, as the centre back warned he would stop his friend by any means necessary. It was set to be war, with van Persie replying that the pair might have grown up but for 90 minutes he would not know Loovens.

Robert Pires struck twice as Arsenal ran out comfortable 2-1 winners, with van Persie involved in the build-up to the second goal. Only the woodwork denied van Persie a goal as his thumping header from a Pires cross should have brought a goal. The pair joked after the game that Loovens would be paying for dinner the next time they dined out as he ran out on the losing side.

It emerged days later that Loovens' no-nonsense message had obviously filtered through to his team mates – van Persie was diagnosed with a broken toe. He had been unaware of the damage leaving the ground but the problem became apparent in the next few days. It had apparently broken after van Persie's foot was innocently trodden on and he did not notice anything untoward.

He was struggling to roll with the punches in the English game and after suffering that broken toe, van Persie revealed some of the underhand tactics that had been used against him in his first season at the club: 'Against Stoke last year, I was playing against one of their defenders and every time I was near him he would keep pinching my skin below my ribs, all the time. And as he was stepping on my toes and yelling in my ear, I was thinking: "What's going on?" I was covered in bruises the next day. We didn't swap shirts either!'

The Premier League was famed for its uncompromising all-action style and although Wenger liked to play his own unique brand of football, he would have to accept his sides would come up against intense opposition most weeks. Teams like Stoke and Blackburn had their critics but that would not make them go away and there would always be some teams who posed a physical threat in the Premier League. Players after a more measured, calm afternoon stroll need not apply – there was plenty of less physically-intense football being played in the likes of Spain's La Liga and the Italian Serie A. Maybe that is why the Ajax and Feyenoord fans saw fit to fight it out in the stands – the battles were not being carried out by their heroes on the pitch.

With the news that Wenger had bought another striker – Emmanuel Adebayor – in the January transfer window, van Persie seemed unfazed. He pointed out that a lot of big clubs needed at least five strikers and he had great belief in his own ability on the pitch. Van Persie told *Arsenal* magazine that he was in it for the long haul at Arsenal: 'I can be important for this club, I think I've proved that a bit, but I'm determined to prove it for the longer term. I've been pleased with the way I've played this season but a lot of people help me here. I have some great examples of how I wanted to change here at Arsenal.'

He bounced back from that broken toe to score a sublime free-kick in the League Cup semi-final second leg at home to Wigan. That magnificent effort was in vain as Jason Roberts struck late on to send Wigan through to their first ever major final. It was a shame the night had to end in disappointment because this was yet another cracking strike from van Persie. By now he was regularly featuring on the BBC *Match of the Day* 'Goal of the Month' competition and his efforts were making Arsenal tickets look like increasingly good value.

The effort came from a long way outside the penalty area and left his old friend Mike Pollitt with no hope in the Wigan goal. The young keeper could only stand and watch as the ball flew into the top corner and he angrily thumped the ball away when it bounced back out of the net. The Sky Sports commentary team instantly labelled the strike 'another classic' but as van Persie ran away it looked like he needed to do some work on a proper goal celebration routine. He threw in as many moves as possible as first he kissed both hands and held his arms outstretched. Next the arms were pumped before he jumped and performed a good old fist-pump. It looked like a gymnast trying to score extra points by putting all their best moves together when next he brought both arms back aloft and cockily nodded his head before pumping his right arm towards the crowd and then being mobbed by team mates.

The free-kick might have been a highlight on a personal level, but the team were knocked out of the League Cup and another chance to claim silverware in their last Highbury season had gone up in smoke.

Bolton Wanderers piled on the misery for Wenger's men as they were dumped out of the FA Cup by the Trotters just four days later. It could have been a lot different if van Persie's header from a Ljungberg cross had been a few inches lower. The pair did not speak to each other off the pitch, according to a book released by Ashley Cole after he left the club for Chelsea, but they were combining well against Bolton. He had rattled the woodwork countless times throughout the season and once again the ball hit the crossbar.

In the last minute it was the slightly more animated figure of Bolton substitute Nicky Hunt that denied van Persie. Just as he looked set to pull the trigger to tie the game, the defender slid in to clear. The BBC *Match of the Day* team had a good giggle at van Persie's expense after he attempted to shoot with that unfavoured right foot. As he swung his right leg forward, he completely missed the ball and ended up on his backside. As former Liverpool defender Alan Hansen remarked, it was 'just one of those things'.

Wenger was left to rue the cruel defeats his team had suffered and said there was no way his team should have lost to Bolton because Stelios' goal was the only decent opportunity Sam Allardyce's battlers had created all game long.

They were on a terrible spell and Arsenal lurched to another crisis in the form of a 3-2 league defeat to West Ham. It was the 2,000th game at Highbury and the Hammers would become the last away team to triumph at the famous old ground. It was not for want of trying on van Persie's behalf as he saw a free-kick nudged away from danger by old head Shaka Hislop after a wonderful slice of build-up play had seen his shot find – you guessed it – the post in its way.

Van Persie needed some inspiration to get him through this lean spell and who better to sit down to dinner with than Dennis Bergkamp? They spent a lot of time together on the pitch and during training sessions but the old head was such a perfectionist that he had no time for idle chit-chat during training sessions. He was so untouchable in training, van Persie joked, that it was impossible to catch him out with a wayward pass, as the Dutch legend would always get the ball under control. He had done a lot of growing up but van Persie still had his cheeky side very much intact.

Away from Arsenal was the only time he was likely to get some advice from Bergkamp and van Persie was thrilled to have gone out to dinner with his team mate with the duo's wives also in attendance. Van Persie chirped: 'You should listen to him, he's clever. He thinks about football every day. I'm really fortunate to learn from a guy like that. He has no ego. He has everyone's respect because of his charisma and the young guys on the training pitch – he has us eating out of his hand.'

As the time came for Arsenal to travel to Real Madrid for the first leg of their Champions League knockout round fixture, some horrible memories came flooding back to van Persie. He had been dropped from the Feyenoord side to face Madrid in the UEFA Super Cup showpiece game after coach-turned-nemesis Bert van Marwijk had taken against van Persie's body language.

It was understandable that van Persie was desperate to play in this game, if only to spite van Marwijk. He had even cut a hole in his boot to accommodate the incredibly swollen broken toe. In the end he was forced to miss the game because, with the best will in the world, he could not even fit his foot inside the boot – even after that special hole had been cut. Despite being stuck in something of a rut since Christmas, Arsenal won the first leg 1-0 at the Bernabéu. With van Persie still missing, they held Madrid to a 0-0 draw at Highbury to put the side containing all-time greats Zinedine Zidane, Raul and Iker Casillas out of the competition.

It looked like clouds were shifting over Highbury and they certainly were for van Persie as he was free from constant threat of charge from Dutch courts. Finally, on Tuesday 28 February – a massive 260 days after his arrest – rape charges against Robin van Persie were dropped. A court was told that it would not be possible to prosecute because there was a lack of evidence available.

A statement from the Dutch prosecutor's office read: 'The inquiry's conclusion is that there is insufficient proof that non-consensual sexual acts took place. At first he denied having sexual contact. But in light of statements from others involved that didn't seem credible, and he admitted to sexual contact, confirming the words of the accused.'

Whilst he would have been jubilant at being free from the threat of prosecution, he did not exactly come out of the matter smelling of roses. He had denied any sexual contact with the girl but had later gone back on that original statement and admitted sleeping with her. Arsenal was a family club and a player who had cheated on his wife would never regain the respect of some of its supporters.

With the case over, van Persie was finally free to break his silence over the 'disgusting' way he was treated by police. He said: 'I did not do anything wrong, I suffered because a woman wanted to make money. And the police have completely messed this one up. I just want people to realise that they have made a huge mistake. They've treated me terribly wrong. All they wanted was to set a high-profile football player as an example for rapists. I can understand that, but when you do that you need to have a strong case.'

Van Persie implied he was only ever accused of the crime because Sandra Boma Krijgsman was one of those women out to make money for herself. This concurred with Bouchra's earlier accusation that Krijgsman wanted to find fame and fortune in a similar way that Rebecca Loos had done after claiming she had a relationship with David Beckham.

Van Persie said: 'I know that people always have their own ideas when players get involved with women. But I do want to make it clear once and for all that there is a certain category of women out there who are looking for money. I was accused of the most horrific things. I was on the news, the whole world had a go at me.

'Knowing my position, who I am and what I do for a living, why on earth would I rape someone? I kept quiet for 10 months, but I do think I had the right to tell my side of the story. This has bothered me for such a long time. I have said what I wanted to say. It is my truth.'

It had been a frustrating break from action with that broken toe but van Persie finally got back into action with two months of the season remaining. Van Persie and crocked star defender Sol Campbell both made their comebacks in a 1-0 behind-closed-doors win over Brighton.

Van Persie made his first-team comeback as Arsenal cruised to a 3-0 Highbury win over Charlton. Originally a bit slow off the mark, he was cheaply dispossessed on several occasions before Gilberto Silva kindly smashed a shot against his back. He finally got a grip on the game and seized on a loose touch from Chris Perry but his attempt to shoot was thwarted by Hermann Hreidarsson, who made a timely interception.

Arsenal were hitting their stride at just the right time as they beat Juventus 2-0 in the first leg of the Champions League quarter-final. Patrick Vieira faced his old club for the first time since leaving and gave Arsenal little to worry about in a quiet performance that saw him yellow-carded. The Italian league leaders were wild in the tackle and had two men sent off. Poor old van Persie was clattered by

Mauro Camoranesi, who was quite rightly sent off. Van Persie was an unused substitute as the Gunners held out for a 0-0 draw in Turin in the second leg to progress to the semi-final stage.

The Dutchman was back among the scorers as Aston Villa were stuffed 5-0 at Highbury. After a through ball, van Persie ran into the box, but as he sped past the advancing Thomas Sørensen, he was wide of the goal and only just managed to stop the ball from going out for a goal kick. As he rolled the ball away from the goal-line to create a more favourable angle for himself, van Persie was joined on the scene by Sørensen and two defenders. The goalkeeper dived at his feet and nearly got a glove on the ball but van Persie teasingly tapped it away from his grasp with his right boot and the ball rolled right in front of Sørensen's nose before he swept the ball home with that trusty left peg.

Manchester United proved they still had the upper hand over Arsenal with a convincing 2-0 win. Van Persie had not performed too badly, forcing compatriot Edwin van der Sar into two decent saves before the home side over-ran them at Old Trafford. As the Premier League season drew to a close the Gunners were in a fight with rivals Tottenham over fourth place in the table – a place that provided a place in next season's Champions League.

Some inventive link play from van Persie saw West Brom beaten 3-1 on 'Dennis Bergkamp Day' at Highbury – fans turned up in orange clothing to thank the retiring ace for all he had done for the club. If he was to stay at Arsenal as long as Bergkamp, perhaps van Persie would one day be recognised in a similar way.

The club legend scored after coming off the bench late on to secure the points and Wenger was full of praise. He said: 'We needed his vision and somebody who could keep the fluency going. That's why I replaced van Persie with him. It had nothing to do with it being Dennis' day.'

It was once again a place on the bench for van Persie as Arsenal beat Villarreal 1-0 in their Champions League semi-final first leg. This was the last ever European game at Highbury and it was a happy night, with Arsenal running out winners and keeping a clean sheet to avoid a costly away goal. With only 10 minutes on the field in a tight affair, there was little for van Persie to add and he did not see a lot of action. He would have been disappointed to be an unused substitute in the second leg, but had a chance of playing some part in a Champions League final after Jens Lehmann's last-minute penalty save secured the 0-0 draw that saw them through.

Tottenham took a point home in their goody bag from the incident-packed party that was the last ever North London derby at Highbury. The managers fell out, the supporters fell out and even the directors fell out as the players cancelled each other out. With Arsenal 1-0 up, van Persie spurned a glorious chance to double the lead and his wastefulness was punished as Robbie Keane tucked away Spurs' equaliser just minutes later. It was a glorious chance to score as he was put through one-on-one with Paul Robinson but unfortunately his shot didn't only go wide of the goalkeeper but also the goal itself.

That wasteful end to a bit-part season continued when van Persie wasted a similar opportunity after coming on as a late substitute in a 3-0 win over Sunderland. Bergkamp cleverly set him clear but van Persie dragged his shot badly wide of the target. This kind of form would hardly have put him top of Wenger's list of starters in the upcoming Champions League final showdown with Barcelona in Paris.

Van Persie put in a terrible performance in Arsenal's win at Manchester City as he seemed more interested in picking a fight with anybody who would listen than in getting on with his football. It had been one of those days for van Persie as his 10th-minute effort smashed against the crossbar and away to safety. David James was equal to his other effort and van Persie had nothing left in his locker.

Something had clearly got under his skin and a petulant van Persie made a gesture to the Eastland crowd as he marched from the field after being hauled off by Wenger. Thierry Henry later said van Persie had been immature after some City fans had given him grief following a first-half storm in a tea cup-type incident.

After the game it emerged that van Persie had been accused of racism by Blues defender David Sommeil. The pair had confronted each other after a routine penalty area marking tussle in the first half and referee Graham Poll had spoken to both players on the pitch and club representatives at half-time.

Just as he had waved goodbye to one set of accusations, another came and landed on his doorstep. After this latest question mark over his character, it was understandable that van Persie made no impact when he came off the bench for the final 10 minutes of Arsenal's last ever match at Highbury. He had been on level pegging with Thierry Henry earlier in the season but by the end of term he had paled in comparison to the talismanic Frenchman, who hit a hat-trick in a 4-2 win. Henry kissed the Highbury turf goodbye as the club looked forward to starting next season in their new Emirates Stadium home.

Neither van Persie or Dennis Bergkamp would go on to play a part in that Champions League final clash with Barcelona, with the surprise name on the score sheet being that of Sol Campbell. The unstoppable defender put his side ahead with a powerful first-half header but things did not work out in his team's favour. Lehmann had been the side's hero in the semi-final but he would turn villain in Paris with an early red card as the Spanish side ran out 2-1 winners.

Lehmann's red card condemned van Persie and Bergkamp to a watching brief as Wenger had one less outfield position to tinker with. He might not have played the biggest part in Arsenal's route to the final but it was still devastating for van Persie to not get on the pitch. After the game he said: 'The final in Paris was a double disappointment. I knew I was not going to start, but I was convinced I'd get on in the second half – but the red card for Jens Lehmann spoilt everything.'

CHAPTER 5

GERMANY AWAITS

I t had ended up as a far from perfect season after that inspiring Christmas period had promised so much. Marco van Basten still thought van Persie had done enough to warrant a place in his provisional Netherlands squad for the 2006 World Cup in Germany. After the disappointment of missing the Champions League final, the Netherlands coach allowed van Persie an extra week off before joining up with the squad. He wanted the player to link up fresh as a daisy, not with stress and angst on his mind. That certainly paid off for the Dutch coach as van Persie joined the fold with an ambitious glint in his eye and trained like a man possessed. Phillip Cocu said that he had been excellent and likened his arrival to 'seeing thunder and lightning in a blue sky'.

That terrific relationship with the national coach was probably one of the reasons he was chosen to represent the Netherlands. Van Persie was thoroughly grateful of the backing van Basten had given him throughout the ordeals of the previous summer and said: 'One of the people who gave me tremendous support was Dutch national boss Marco van Basten. I knew myself that one day the truth would come out, but it took a long time before police and a court in Holland admitted that they were wrong.'

Van Persie looked something like back to his best in the Netherlands' warm-up game against Cameroon where he creatively carved open several chances from the right-hand side. Ruud van Nistelrooy scored the game's only goal after van Persie caught the eye with a string of intelligent passes and weaving runs on the ball. He did however make a couple of rash challenges for a friendly match, which did not bode well for the finals.

He would have to learn to accept that at international level you had to play at whatever position you were put, no matter where you are used to playing for your club. Van Persie found himself out on the right wing for this game as Marco van Basten tested the water to see how he would be able to switch the team around during the World Cup. The coach said he adapted to the position 'very well' playing wide on the right flank. Whilst Germany and Portugal were scoring for fun, van Basten said it was important for players to learn different formations in friendly games. A team able to adapt is more likely to be one able to survive.

In a warm-up friendly against Mexico van Basten switched the side around again and van Persie was placed up front in a 2-1 win. The coach was again insistent it had been a worthwhile exercise as he tried out different formations the side might need to adopt later on. It might have looked to the pundits that the Netherlands were not totally prepared for their opening World Cup game just 10 days away but van Basten was insistent he needed to be able to shuffle the side. Van Persie would have been confident of getting a game because van Basten looked confident in his ability to play in a variety of roles.

Lucas Neill knew all about van Persie ahead of his Australia side's friendly match against the Dutch. Blackburn defender Neill had witnessed some of van Persie's finest performances in an Arsenal shirt – the Dutchman had passed him on the way to scoring that double at the Millennium Stadium the previous year. After also watching van Persie's wonderful solo goal at Highbury that season he said: 'Van Persie is up and coming, very strong and very sharp. He has got a great left foot and is a fantastic player.'

That willingness to adapt to several different positions pleased the coach and van Persie was suddenly almost guaranteed a spot in the side by van Basten. He confirmed that with future Spurs star Rafael van der Vaart ruled out with injury, van Persie would be the team's first-choice free-kick taker. He said: 'You come to the conclusion that van Persie is so good that it would be a shame not to use him.'

It was no accident that Robin van Persie was able to play on the right – he had worked on using his right foot since joining Arsenal in order to be able to play on that side. His left foot was the star of the show but after working on the right one for months he was now able to play well with both feet. With his national team, van Persie had more freedom to express himself than in the precise passing machine of Arsenal. He said: 'Van Basten gives me a lot of freedom to do things on the pitch. At Arsenal I am more a passer of the ball. There are two van Persies now, the one at Arsenal and the one with Holland; two different players.'

The frame of the goal had become van Persie's greatest nemesis during the season just gone and he was reunited with that old friend in the 1-1 draw with Australia. The Netherlands' World Cup free-kick taker looked like finding his range and after beating Mark Schwarzer all ends up he heard that familiar 'ping' sound and the ball bounced away to safety. It was a terrible way for the Netherlands to prepare as Wesley Sneijder, Phillip Cocu and Giovanni van Bronckhorst were all injured by uncompromising Aussie tackles. Australia were a disgrace for conducting themselves in such a manner on the eve of the world's most important tournament. Luke Wilkshire was shown the red card for a rash challenge as the referee did his best to prevent a full-scale riot.

With gaps to fill, van Persie paid for his versatility by being dragged back to bolster an underweight midfield. The Australians had savaged the team and van Persie must have been relieved to come through the match unscathed himself. After his injury problems of the previous season, his body might have been becoming a bit more fragile and susceptible to problems.

Marco van Basten was having the same injury problems as a manger that had plagued his playing career. But he was fit for Euro 1988 where he'd scored a scorching volley as the Netherlands won what is so far their only major trophy. He had the relevant experience to pass to van Persie for a major tournament. First choice players were dropping like flies but van Persie might have had a little more in the tank after missing a chunk of the season with niggling injuries and that broken toe. This was a big opportunity if he was able to grab it – he was surely now their most important link between midfield and attack.

Van Persie was relatively young at 22 but players with less experience had done brilliantly on the big stage – Michael Owen made a name for himself at the 1998 World Cup when he capped a fine tournament with a memorable solo effort against Argentina. The Dutch press were incredibly excited by van Persie's promising contribution in those warm-up games and he was being compared to English wonder-kid Wayne Rooney, who had burst onto the scene at just 17 and starred for his country.

The national coach was certainly full of praise for his whizz-kid, saying he was in superb form. Van Basten said that although it was early days, he was excited to see van Persie showing so much promise in the warm-up games and that he was showing real class. He was also delighted to see that calm head prevent van Persie from listening to the hype: 'Van Persie refuses to get carried away by the hero-grams heading his way', said the coach.

There was little danger of van Persie getting carried away by what was said about him in the press because he ignored it all. His name had been dragged through the mud in the past and he was not interested in what the media had to say at all. A lot of players pretend they do not know what has been said but van Persie really didn't – when newspapers revealed Dennis Bergkamp had signed a contract extension at Arsenal, van Persie had shocked reporters when he revealed he did not know about the deal because nobody had told him.

It had been pointed out that the Netherlands had a very

young squad but there were a few old heads thrown in to steady the ship. The more experienced Edwin van der Sar, Phillip Cocu and Edgar Davids had seen it all before and were likely to prove invaluable to the younger lads like van Persie who would have needed a quiet word in their ears at one point or another.

Van Persie said being a young squad was a non-issue and the kids had already proved their ability with that fine qualification campaign where they had won the majority of matches and were unbeaten. He reasoned that the Arsenal squad had featured a lot of youngsters that season but after Wenger had instilled belief in them, the side made it to the final of the Champions League.

It was just a case of waiting to see where van Basten would fit him into the side. So, just a year after that prison officer had kindly told Robin van Persie he would never play for his country again, he was set to be one of their most important players at a World Cup finals tournament. All the hype was over and finally it was time to get down to business.

The Dutch had a relatively easy opening game against Serbia and Montenegro, who lacked creativity but had a steely resolve that would take some beating. They were set for another afternoon of crunching tackles – maybe that preparation clash with Australia had been a good idea after all.

In the end van Basten's favoured formation saw Ruud van Nistelrooy up front with Arjen Robben on the left and van Persie on the right. The wingers would cut in and act as strikers when the side were on the attack. It was a good thing van Persie had been working on that right foot as he was going to need it.

Van Persie had a dream start to the World Cup when he set up the winning goal with just 17 minutes on the clock. When a seemingly innocuous ball bounced in the centre circle, van Persie spotted an opening and whipped an accurately weighted lob beyond the backline for the onrushing Arjen Robben to collect. The Chelsea forward was on to it like a flash and before you could say 'Slobodan Miloševi', Serbia and Montenegro were behind. It was a neat finish as Robben stroked the ball home but the goal was all about the vision of van Persie picking out the initial pass. Robben may have taken the plaudits but van Basten would surely have been impressed with the way things had started for van Persie.

Club rivalries were forgotten as the Chelsea man was mobbed by van Persie and United's Ruud van Nistelrooy after it appeared his joy was so great that he could not stay on his feet. There was no sign of the Netherlands' usual dressing room tensions as the players rushed to congratulate Robben.

That united picture painted on the pitch disappeared once the game was over, however, as van Persie somewhat crazily accused Robben of being a selfish player. It seemed an odd move to make at the start of a tournament, more the kind of observation a player should make once it has finished. Maybe van Persie became jealous after Robben received rave reviews after scoring the winner that he had set up.

Van Persie fumed after the game that there was no 'I' in Netherlands: 'Together we hope to play six matches and he can't do it all by himself. He must take into account his team mates. Sometimes, he makes decisions for himself and not the team.'

After displaying versatility in the warm-up games, van Persie had found a way into the starting line-up. Out on the right he now faced playing second fiddle to Robben as a result; he later moved into the middle of the park but would still have preferred to be on the left. On reflection he was better off playing on the right than not at all but he was still frustrated by watching the Chelsea man star in what he felt was his position. Robben boasted that fans had seen nothing of him yet, whilst van Basten was worrying that there was a lot more squabbling to come as well as good football.

The coach was keen not to take sides and did his best to present a united picture in the camp. He said both men had been right in what they had said and highlighted the importance of teamwork in their effort.

He added: 'We discussed a little bit with the two players and also we said something about a situation like that in general to the whole team. Arjen did very good work with the ball and maybe the players felt that during the game. The next game it is going to be the case for van Persie.'

The pair put on a united front at training a couple of days later when Robben told reporters he knew there was no malice in van Persie's words and the comments were not an issue at all. Unsurprisingly, van Persie claimed his words had been taken out of context and the media had once again made a mountain out of a molehill. He was still insistent the Dutch would have to play as a team to succeed in the tournament. They looked happy enough together during the training session but it was quite possible that yet another rift had started that could see the Netherlands side fall out as squads had done in previous years.

Arsène Wenger commented amongst claim and counter-claim by supporters of Robben that young players were right to go for goal. He told the *Evening Standard*: 'Sometimes young players shoot when they should pass the ball – but if you do not try it then you do not score.'

Lyon manager Gérard Houllier knew all about the Premier League from his spell in charge of Liverpool that had ended in 2004, and he was impressed with the way van Persie had fitted into this somewhat unfamiliar role on the right. He said that van Persie had done well to fit into a pattern that he was not used to and could be a driving force in the tournament.

It was hard to predict what the Netherlands would come up against when they faced the Ivory Coast. The African side was not afraid to chop and change tactics and formations so van Basten would need to be prepared for a range of scenarios. Van Persie and Robben must have been wondering if their positions were under threat but van Basten said he would not sacrifice the duo no matter how the 'Elephants' lined up.

Van Basten was right when he said this game would be van Persie's time to shine as he starred in a 2-1 win in Stuttgart that saw the Dutch qualify for the second round. Van Persie opened the scoring with his first World Cup goal – and what a goal it was. Both wingers posed an early threat by cutting in from the flanks and when van Persie cut in from the right, his pace was too much for Arsenal team mate Kolo Touré to handle and the bulky defender pole-axed him. They may have known each other well but all bets were off when the two crossed the white line. Touré brought van Persie's run to a premature end with a crunching tackle that saw van Persie take a knock to his right thigh. After the tournament Touré said van Persie had been terrific and in a way it was a big compliment to hack him down in the game because it highlighted how much of a problem van Persie's pace was for the Africans.

It was another bruising affair against the Ivory Coast and injury was surely only just around the corner for one of the Dutch players. Shaken but not stirred, van Persie picked himself up and as he prepared to take the resulting free-kick, casually adjusted his collar with all the swagger of James Bond himself. The free-kick was positioned pretty centrally and was not too far outside the penalty area so van Persie lined up that left foot and shaped to shoot, with Arjen Robben looking on jealously. Finally van Persie had wrestled centre stage away from the left winger and it was his time to shine. He swept in a glorious shot that was so perfectly measured it went inches over the heads of the Ivory Coast wall and crashed its way into the top left-hand corner of the goal before the Elephants' keeper Jean-Jacques Tizie could do anything about it.

Team mates mobbed him after a perfect goal that said 'I can do it too'. The Africans staged a strong second-half comeback and van Persie was the hero at the other end of the pitch to deny them a certain goal. With goalkeeper van der Sar beaten by a strong header from a corner, van Persie was there on the line to chest Chelsea man Didier Drogba's bullet header away from danger. He showed good technique by making sure both hands were behind him to prevent an accidental handball.

After the game van Persie revealed that was something the Dutch had worked on in training: 'We work on situations like that a lot in training, so it was my job to be on the line to clear it. But it was a difficult situation because the ball was bouncing up towards my shoulder. I just had to stay calm and react properly.'

The term 'legend' is bounded about all too often but Johan Cruyff was a man worthy of such praise. The Dutch hero was at the game and went to find van Persie to congratulate him after the match. Van Persie was predictably delighted with reaching the next round and scoring that absolute scorcher of a free-kick. He said: 'We worked hard. We played well at times, we should be proud that we reached the next round. I am not sure what meant more, my goal or my clearance. My goal was fantastic for us all.'

Tottenham manager Martin Jol had been impressed with van Persie's performances against Spurs earlier in the season and he had similar thoughts after watching the Dutch victory. He said: 'I thought van Persie was marvellous. Johan Cruyff said he was the strongest physically, and that's an unbelievable compliment, because before he went to England, van Persie was regarded as a little weak.'

That bulking up in his first couple of seasons at Arsenal had clearly paid off. Van Persie had moved on considerably from the delicate flower that had joined from Feyenoord. With a strong performance in this second match he showed defenders he was not afraid to make his mark and, like a cactus plant, it was not advisable to run into him.

Inevitably there had been plenty of banter on the Arsenal training ground between van Persie and Ivory Coast men Kolo Touré and Emmanuel Eboué but van Persie said he was sad to see the African side eliminated from the tournament and his friends go home.

Argentina had also already qualified for the second round, so it was in some senses a meaningless final group match in Frankfurt. There was however a slightly easier game in store for the winners of the group as they would play a distinctly average Mexican side in the second round. Van Persie suggested both teams would be more relaxed but that it was still an important one to win in terms of taking confidence into the second round. If one of the teams could win this game they would have reason to be extremely confident of getting very far in the tournament. Argentina were a frightening proposition as they had won their last game 5-0 with the Dutch team watching in a mixture of amazement and fear. 'I just thought "Oh Jesus!"' van Persie joked.

The game turned out to be the damp squib those in possession of tickets had feared it would be. It was completely understandable that neither team wanted to wear themselves out or reveal too much about the possible dangers they posed. The game ended in a goalless draw with neither goalkeeper being bothered too much. Hopefully van Persie was saving his best for later in the tournament as he put in a display that was average at best. He offered little creativity going forward, showed surprisingly poor control when it was needed the most and fired a free-kick well wide.

After all that talk of what a great manager Marco van Basten was, after he had bent over backwards to help van Persie, he completely lost the plot after the Argentina game. It was typical of the Netherlands for the squad to spontaneously combust and it looked like they were going to do so again at the Germany World Cup.

Ruud van Nistelrooy had hardly been having the tournament of a lifetime but had found the back of the net, and it was a surprise when van Basten told a press conference that he was not good enough and would not be playing their next game – the second round match against Portugal. This was terrible news for van Persie because his chances of winning the World Cup had effectively gone up in smoke. The wing men had worked well behind van Nistelrooy so far and surely the threesome were going to become a more effective force as the tournament progressed.

There must have been a private falling-out as van Basten announced that van Nistelrooy was not good enough technically to represent the Netherlands. He qualified the argument by saying he had pulled the striker off during all three games they had played so far and so he could not have been content with the way he was playing.

Van Basten told the shocked reporters: 'We have two great players on the wing, don't tell me the service from them is not good enough. Robin van Persie and Arjen Robben are in great form. It's true that Ruud is marked by good defenders in this World Cup, but he should be used to that.'

This would have unsettled the squad and in particular van Persie, who did not cope well with managers who were not nice to their players.

Van Persie himself had been attracting rave reviews for his performances. French attacking midfielder Robert Pires had left Arsenal just before the tournament started but was full of praise for van Persie. Pires said his former team mate had the important quality of perseverance and had improved greatly as a player in the two seasons they played together. He said it was strange that van Persie had not been a regular starter for Arsenal but was starting every game for his country. This was a good point but maybe it had something to do with the style that the different teams played in. With Wenger's team featuring both Bergkamp and Henry upfront, there was less space for an attacking winger to cut in like Robben and van Persie had been doing for the Dutch.

Wenger liked to see his players as projects and played the long game, whereas it is a different ball game for national coaches who have to do the best with what they have at their disposal in the present and do not really have to worry about the long term. In less important games van Persie had been played upfront and Wenger planned to convert him into a striker, but in the short term van Persie had little chance of being a first-choice striker at Arsenal.

Pires recognised the hard work van Persie had put in to develop his right foot – something that had resulted in him playing at this World Cup. He told the *Sunday Times*: 'It is important for a winger to be two-footed, although it's still very rare to see a player who is perfectly two-footed and probably rarer to find a left-footed player who looks as strong with his right. It tends to happen the other way around. That's part of the charm of the left-hander, or left-footer, in sport. I imagine that coach Marco van Basten wants him to take advantage of his shooting ability when he moves inside.'

Not a lot had been said about the fact that van Persie was a top player with an amazing left foot when a lot of players were stronger with their right. Pires said it was a great aspect of van Persie's game because he would hit the ball at angles other players would find it impossible to make. He likened van Persie's delivery to the shots of the tennis ace Rafael Nadal, who was left-handed and was able to find 'impossible' angles.

It all fell apart for the Dutch in the meeting with Portugal as Maniche's wonder-goal won the game for Luiz Felipe Scolari's side. They struggled to find any rhythm to their game in van Nistelrooy's absence and the Portuguese were just a bit more at the races.

To say this was a bad-tempered affair would be the understatement of the century, as the two teams kicked lumps out of each other. It was such an intensely fought match that it would later be dubbed 'The Battle of Nuremberg'. Both sides had two men sent off in a game that equalled a World Cup record with four red cards and an amazing sixteen yellow cards. Surprisingly, van Persie was not one of the players to receive a card – if riled he could be something of a loose cannon.

Van Persie struggled to get a foothold in the game and did not have too much involvement. He did well early on to dance in between two defenders but he shot well wide after getting a glimpse of goal. There was more of the same later after a moment of brilliance left Ricardo Carvalho and Nuno Valente biting the dirt when they both slid in for the ball only for van Persie to drag it back out of their paths, but once again his shot was wayward. A later long-distance shot never looked like troubling the net as the Dutch attack looked all out of ideas. The one time he looked like scoring, Portugal's Costinha decided ridiculously to stick out an arm and block the pass, earning himself an early bath in the process.

It was a real shame to see a campaign that had started off

quite well end on such a sour note, and with van Persie not being at the races. He had scored the best free-kick at the tournament but performed somewhat inconsistently under the challenging circumstances of an unpredictable coach and dressing room tensions.

He made the relatively short journey home and soon it was time for van Persie to start concentrating on Arsenal again. With Dennis Bergkamp swapping his boots for pipe and slippers, it was a period of change in the Gunners attack and van Persie needed to be on his game to cement a place in the side.

He faced stiff competition with José Antonio Reyes, Emmanuel Adebayor, Tomáš Rosický and wonder kid Theo Walcott all after that spot next to Thierry Henry. Van Persie said all the advice and encouragement Bergkamp had given him left him well-equipped for the battle that lay ahead: 'He helped me a lot, sometimes I think I was asking him too much and asking all types of things. When I see how he lives, it's a great example – he's a different human being. The way he does it is fantastic on and off the pitch.'

Mahatma Gandhi said people should be the change they want to see in the world and that was very much the case with van Persie. He had come to Arsenal as a talented but troubled young man and observed one of his childhood heroes up close and personal. After two years of studying, it was van Persie's time to step up to the mark and become Arsenal's new star centre forward.

He looked sharp in pre-season action for the Gunners and grabbed a brace as Austrians SK Schwadorf were trounced 8-1. After a neat one-two with Reyes, van Persie made the goalkeeper look a clown with an audacious dummy to open the scoring. In the second half he turned predator to bury Alexander Hleb's cross into the net before a defender could react. The club's World Cup stars made their comebacks in this low-profile game as once again Wenger's perfect scheduling kept the pressure off returning players to avoid any mishaps or flash points. A late penalty in a friendly at AZ Alkmaar would have shown Wenger that van Persie meant business this year and was ready to weigh in with his fair share of goals.

Van Persie had very clear goals set out for the upcoming season. He told the *Express* that consistency was the key if he was to become a more useful player. He had always been good in fits and starts but was not exactly the kind of player that Wenger would have been able to count on for a big performance on a regular basis. He said: 'Every game I play I have to stand out. I don't want to be satisfied with a supporting role and a goal now and again. I have to give my colleagues the feeling I can be decisive for them. We are aiming for the highest and the team is strong enough to do it.

Arsenal had a few injury problems for the first of their two-legged Champions League group stage qualifying tie with Dynamo Zagreb and there were suggestions they might come unstuck against the Croatians. Van Persie fired a warning shot that the Gunners were not to be messed with and had not been sidetracked by off-the-field events, saying: 'We all know how important the game is and we will not let anything distract us.'

Robin van Persie was born on the same date as actress Barbara Windsor and two days after celebrating his 23rd birthday he netted in a 3-0 first-leg win to make sure it was a case of 'Carry on in Europe'. Van Persie's strike, sandwiched between a Cesc Fàbregas double, saw him smartly drill the ball home after running onto a well-timed Hleb through ball. In a brilliant display van Persie also set up the opener for Fàbregas when he slipped in the Spaniard from his position on the right.

Wenger was delighted with the way his young side had dealt with the pressure of the situation – those goals were like gold dust as qualifying for the group stages was worth millions of pounds. The Frenchman was then left fuming as a round of international friendlies interfered with the start to the season. The Netherlands steamrolled the Republic of Ireland 4-0 with van Persie netting the final goal after a masterclass from new boy Klaas-Jan Huntelaar. The new kid on the block slipped in van Persie, whose powerful shot clipped the underside of the bar and went in. Last season, that would have bounced out of play. Something had definitely changed.

Former Arsenal man Robert Pires had played with van Persie for two seasons and said he was sure van Persie would get the chance to play more games in the upcoming season. He warned that the Dutchman would have to be at his best to get a decent run in the side because Wenger had assembled an impressive bunch of attacking players.

Pires told the *Sunday Times*: 'I imagine we will see him more and more with Arsenal, although Wenger may have some problems next season with so many strong players wanting to fill the attacking positions: Van Persie, Emmanuel Adebayor, Tomáš Rosický, Freddie Ljungberg, José Antonio Reyes and Alexander Hleb. All of them can work with Thierry Henry. Doubtless the manager has some thoughts on how to work it out.'

Arsenal came from behind to draw their first game at the new £390 million Emirates stadium after Gilberto Silva buried a cross from 17-year-old new signing Theo Walcott. Van Persie was restricted to a watching brief before coming on in the 65th minute and nearly connecting with Walcott's cross which his Brazilian team mate eventually buried.

It was frustrating for van Persie to be on the bench for his club after starting every game for his country at the World Cup. Wenger understood he might have been upset but explained he needed the 23-year-old fit for upcoming games and reasoned that he would be tired after that victory in Ireland. He said: 'It was a choice between Robin and Thierry on Saturday. I did not play him against Villa because we need him for other games. He had played the whole game for Holland in midweek and it is four games in ten days at the start of the season.'

Arsenal were disappointing in the second leg of their qualifier with Zagreb, trailing for a long period before a van Persie free-kick fed Freddie Ljungberg to level the scores as they ran out 2-1 winners to taste victory at the Emirates for the first time. It was his best Arsenal performance for a long time as van Persie stung the hands of goalkeeper Ivan Turnia and had a goal-bound shot deflected onto the bar by a last-ditch block.

The early signs were not promising for Arsenal's title challenge as they slipped to a 1-0 defeat at Manchester City thanks to a Joey Barton penalty. It was a case of what might have been as van Persie had clipped the inside of the post minutes before the goal and also thought he should have won a penalty kick after being shoved by Richard Dunne as the evening drew to a conclusion. Thierry Henry said after the game he was certain it was a penalty and van Persie was so incensed that he earned himself a booking in his protests.

Arsène Wenger was livid that his side had been denied a point by the decision. He said: 'For me it was a penalty because he lost his man. He stopped him from playing the ball. Richard Dunne was pushing Van Persie in the back, it's a penalty. You can say things even themselves out by the end of the season, but we need refs to get things right on the day.'

With the exits of experienced players Sol Campbell, Robert Pires and a certain Mr Bergkamp that summer, van Persie now found himself one of the elder statesmen of the team and in position to hand out advice to younger players like Walcott. He told the *Independent on Sunday* that it was great to be in this position and he loved playing with talented youngsters like Walcott and Fàbregas: 'I started playing for Feyenoord when I was 18. When I was his age, I wasn't as good as Walcott is now. They're young but it doesn't matter, they're young and good. To me it's a joy to play with players like that. I think guys like Cesc and Theo, you follow them. You see these guys maybe once in 10 years at other clubs. It's really special. They are so young and so excited. We should be happy that they are at this level.'

He had matured and grown as a player in those two years at Arsenal and van Persie recognised the massive part older heads Bergkamp and Campbell had played in that process. It was an upward spiral of learning and van Persie had shown he was keen to help other players in the same way that he had been given advice in the past.

They might not have got off to the best of starts but van Persie said he still believed in Arsenal's ability to challenge for the title. After reigning champions Chelsea also lost he said: 'Hopefully we can play every game at our maximum level and then we will see where it ends. Everything is open and it is good for everybody that Chelsea lost a game.'

Just over two months after they had limped out of the World Cup with that defeat to Portugal, the Netherlands and van Persie were back in competitive action with a Euro 2008 qualifying match. As usual Marco van Basten moved van Persie around the field, starting him on the right wing but later moving him into the centre of the park. It was van Persie's 17th-minute corner that set up Joris Mathijsen for the only goal of the game.

Playing in a free role against Belarus certainly got van Persie's tail up as he netted twice in a dominant performance. The Dutch ran out 3-0 winners as they secured maximum points from the opening round of qualifying matches. He opened the scoring with an unstoppable drive just after the half-hour mark and added a second late on when he scored via the inside of the post before Dirk Kuyt added a third. It could have been a hat-trick had referee Howard Webb decided to award a penalty when van Persie took a tumble in the box.

It had nearly caused a dressing room bust up in the World Cup but van Persie was banging on about playing like a team again after that win. Perhaps it was an attempt to deflect some of the limelight he was given for those two goals onto other members of the team. He said: 'I think what is important was that we played as a team. It was very difficult to play our football, but on a crucial night like this I think we did well.'

It was a brilliant performance for van Persie and things

were looking increasingly rosy in his blossoming career. As he had grown up van Persie had learned to focus on the things that really mattered and put side issues where they belonged. He told the *Daily Express*: 'I have progressed a lot in all kinds of areas – personally, football wise and mentally. I have become stronger, more in balance. And I know how to separate main issues from side issues. When I look at the 17-year-old Robin van Persie and the 23-year-old Robin van Persie I see a world of difference.'

He had spoken about looking out for the younger members of the squad and said that he sometimes saw the bad attitudes that he had possessed in years gone by. He added: 'Sometimes they are a little too busy and spend too much unnecessary energy on side issues. That is what I used to do as well. From experience I know it is totally useless to talk to them. The process of growing up is unexplainable.

'That was the case with me and that would not be different with them. You have to go through it, you have to find out what is good and what is wrong and you figure it out only when you've been through certain situations. That is what happened with me.'

He may have been a more mature figure but van Persie lacked a certain cutting edge as the Gunners again flattered to deceive at their new home. Middlesbrough took a point after the home side had been unable to find their killer touch. The only consistency evident in van Persie's game that day was in his inability to beat big Aussie goalkeeper Mark Schwarzer. With a free-kick heading towards the top corner, the Australia number one dramatically dived across his goal and punched away to safety. As Gareth Southgate's men halted the reds in their tracks, van Persie became increasingly agitated and was lucky to stay on the pitch after a horrifically late lunge on dominant centre back Jonathan Woodgate.

Just like the previous season, Arsenal were not fulfilling their potential in the Premier League but bobbing quite nicely along the Champions League river. They started off their Champions League group stage with a comfortable 2-1 win over Hamburg. After being slipped through by Adebayor, van Persie won his side a penalty thanks to a cheeky piece of skill. After baring down on goal, he faked to shoot and the goalkeeper came clattering in for a stonewall penalty and red card. The captain Gilberto Silva made no mistake from the spot and Tomáš Rosický added another before the Germans pulled one back late on. For the second match in a row a sublime van Persie free-kick was parried away from danger.

After they felt he drew the challenge of goalkeeper Sascha Kirschstein, the Hamburg fans booed van Persie as he made his way off the field when subbed in the 70th minute. He would not have been too fussed as Arsenal went on to win, but Hamburg supporters and players were left fuming after they felt van Persie only took a slight knock from Kirschstein's glove and had exaggerated the incident to get the goalkeeper red carded.

Hamburg coach Thomas Doll suggested van Persie either had bad balance or had cheated his way to the penalty. He moaned: 'I don't think we would have lost with 11 players on the field. Van Persie played the ball too far outside and stepped on Kirschstein's hand and fell.'

It was like water off a duck's back for van Persie who was probably quite bored, having not been involved in a good old controversy for a little while. The ground containing more than 50,000 supporters had turned into a cauldron of hate but his ability to cope with situations like this was one of the reasons Wenger had brought him to the club.

Van Persie was angry at claims he had cheated and he stated it was something he was in fact very much against: 'I wouldn't dive. It's something I don't agree with. It's not good for the game. It may not have been obvious to everyone at the time but I'm sure there was slight contact as I tried to get past the goalkeeper.'

Left-back Ashley Cole had departed the club under acrimonious circumstances in the summer and wrote a book giving his opinion on goings on at his former club. Arsenal had done well to maintain a stiff upper lip as details of his sometimes harsh words emerged in the newspapers and he had claimed the club did not have the same spirit it used to possess. Van Persie could not bear to hear his club being unfairly criticised and broke from the ranks to respond that Cole had written a lot of nonsense.

He said: 'That's nonsense about our spirit. The boss said this is almost the best team he's had and I agree with that. We have a young, talented squad, a good mix. You definitely don't get to the Champions League final without spirit and commitment. That was only a few months ago. Arsenal is a big team. It's one big happy family and of course everyone wants to play.'

This might not have impressed bosses at the club, who had probably instructed players not to comment on the book, but it certainly won him brownie points with the supporters as Cole had become public enemy number one after moving to rivals Chelsea.

After missing the monumental win at Old Trafford with a hip injury, van Persie claimed he was having to work harder than other players to get to where he wanted to be: 'I know this is an important season for me. It is my aim to make myself an important part of this team this year. I always feel I have to work twice as hard as other people to get what I want, and that, in my opinion, sometimes I deserve. It has been like that all my career. That's not a negative thing about the boss or a complaint. That's just how it is. It's something that keeps me focused. I have been here two years. I can understand when you come from a different culture, a different club with different ideas, you have to be patient. But two years is a long time. The boss feels similar, that I'm ready to play now.'

It was clear van Persie felt he was once again battling the odds. He felt that after spending two years honing his craft in North London, he deserved his chance to get a run in the first team. He said that successful and somewhat unexpected run in the Netherlands team at the World Cup was a massive boost. Van Persie badly wanted that regular spot in Wenger's side to help them achieve their big dreams and finally lift another piece of silverware.

He started the 2-0 win over Porto but failed to get on the score sheet after spurning a couple of chances before Thierry Henry showed him how it was done. There just wasn't enough power on his flicked header, which was easily plucked out of the air by Helton. His link play was not up to its usual standard as van Persie uncharacteristically dithered over his passes and Porto were able to stop him from playing effectively.

He had been a little off-colour after that hip injury but

that was all forgotten as van Persie scored one of the goals of the season as he grabbed a brace in the 2-1 win at Charlton Athletic. His first-time volley from 20 yards out rocketed past Scott Carson and into the net to send the Arsenal supporters behind the goal into raptures. It was a sensational goal which was not only very easy on the eye but also the perfect example of how to execute a volley.

Arsenal had been behind to Darren Bent's opener but van Persie equalised with a well-taken goal after Alexander Hleb had done well to find him with a through ball. Van Persie would make that first strike appear distinctly average with his second, the winning goal. Emmanuel Eboué had charged down the right-hand flank and as he started to run out of space, centred the ball more in hope than anything. As the ball dipped down towards the ground outside the penalty area, van Persie leapt and sent the dipping volley from the left-hand side of the box back across Carson and into the top right-hand corner.

Amid mad celebrations he climbed a few steps to go wild with the supporters before Henry joined in with the fun as Arsène Wenger celebrated 10 years in charge of Arsenal in style. It was exactly the kind of expansive, creative and beautiful football that Wenger had cultivated at the club. Van Persie later told the BBC it was the best goal he had scored so far in his career and it meant even more to him because Arsenal had won the game.

But in typical Robin van Persie style, things were not exactly straightforward in a full-blooded affair at The Valley and he was lucky to even be on the pitch after an ugly tackle. Countryman Jimmy-Floyd Hasselbaink felt the full force of a van Persie tackle and the 23-year-old was

Robin van Persie began his football career at boyhood side SBV Excelsior and joined Dutch side Feyenoord Rotterdam as a 16-year-old. He made his debut for the club in 2001.

Above: The young van Persie had many admirers at Feyenoord, but repeatedly clashed with the coaching staff. He was sent home from the 2002 UEFA Super Cup after a rift with coach Bert van Marwijk.

Right: Van Persie joined Arsenal in the summer of 2004 and won a trophy on his debut for the club when the Gunners beat Manchester United 3–1 in the FA Community Shield.

Above: Despite spending the majority of his first full season at Arsenal on the bench, van Persie helped the Gunners progress to the FA Cup final by scoring twice in the semi-final against Blackburn in 2005. The Gunners went on to beat Manchester United in the final at the Millennium Stadium in Cardiff.

Below: The Dutchman was hindered by injury throughout the season, however, and could only contribute five goals to Arsenal's league campaign.

Thierry Henry's departure to Barcelona in the summer of 2007 allowed van Persie to assume the role of main striker at the club. Arsenal finished the 2007/08 campaign third in the Premier League, only three points off champions Manchester United.

Van Persie has amassed
over 50 caps for
Holland and scored
over 20 goals.

Van Persie scored his 50th Arsenal goal in 2008 and in January 2009 every Arsenal goal was either scored or assisted by the Dutchman. He had his best season overall for Arsenal and the club named him Player of the Season.

fortunate to only see a yellow card after all hell broke loose following the clash.

After the game all the talk was about that special second goal, one that Wenger hailed as being a 'once in a lifetime' effort that nobody could have seen coming. He enthused: 'When the ball came over I thought we didn't have anyone in the box and then suddenly van Persie came in at full pace and power. I thought it was going to go over the bar but the technique was perfect. It was definitely one of the best I have seen since I took charge at Arsenal. It was unbelievable.' However Wenger was worried that van Persie had lost his temper after being wound up by Hasselbaink. He knew it could so easily have been another red card, which would have prevented the wonder goal from happening at all. As with that red card at Southampton back at the start of his time at Arsenal, Wenger was pleading with van Persie to calm down and not do anything stupid.

Wenger compared the Man of the Match to a young version of former captain Vieira, who also had something of a temper in his early years. If he could follow the example of the French colossus and stop himself getting so easily infuriated, van Persie could follow Vieira's example. He had been a player with flaws when Wenger bought him, the reason Feyenoord had charged a relatively small transfer fee.

The modest van Persie was quick to praise Eboué for setting up the goal because with a different type of delivery he would not have had the chance to score such a goal. He told the *Daily Star*: 'It was a fantastic cross from Eboué. There was a little bit of a curve on the cross but, when I saw it coming, I was just focused on hitting it straight and at the heart of the ball. When I hit it I thought it was going over but it went down and it was a fantastic moment.'

Referee Mark Clattenburg could have made the afternoon a completely different one had he chosen to send van Persie off for that spat with Hasselbaink, and Wenger also revealed he had thought about taking him off.

Charlton manager Iain Dowie said the strike showed absolutely supreme technique and wished he had been at home applauding the volley rather than sat in the dugout watching his team conceding it. Van Persie had quite rightly stolen the headlines with a fantastic performance that proved that if he could find a bit more consistency, he could easily be Arsenal's best player.

Wenger was extremely irritated to see his players leaving for more international duty. The Dutch were distinctly off-colour in their qualifier in Bulgaria but van Persie nicked them a valuable point after being played at centre forward. Ruud van Nistelrooy should really have been playing there but after his fall-out with Marco van Basten, the versatility of Robin van Persie was once again desperately needed by his country. It was a brilliant response for van Persie to score with his head and his coach later raved that he was a complete player.

The Dutch looked the worst they had done in recent years and would have struggled to get anything from their game with lowly Albania had it not been for another immense van Persie performance. He really looked on top of his game as he once again led from the front by scoring one and forcing Nevil Dede to put through his own net for the second.

Albania had only reached the European Championships

finals once before and put up one hell of a fight with Debatik Curri hitting the back of the net. Van Persie appeared to now be the Netherlands' main goal threat so they would have been relieved to see him slot the ball under the advancing goalkeeper for the opener. It was another technically perfect volley – a bit closer than the much lauded effort against Charlton – that skidded under the goalkeeper after being set up by a series of cushioned headers reminiscent of the kids' street football game 'headers and volleys'.

The Albanians clearly classed van Persie as a massive threat but despite being double-marked when he received the ball, he still managed to weave a route to the penalty area and as he attempted the pull-back, the ball ballooned off Dede and into the goal. Those two proved good enough to get the Dutch back to winning ways but van Persie looked less than impressed as he trudged off at full time. It had always been his message that they needed to play as a team and he would have been angered by the below-par performance put in by some of his colleagues. Unlike Arjen Robben sometimes seemed to, van Persie was definitely not happy to do it all by himself.

After once again starring for his country, van Persie was resigned to the bench for Arsenal's game at home to Watford as Theo Walcott was given his first start for the club. Perhaps Wenger did not want to wear him out but a decision like this sent out all the wrong signals and van Persie would have been slightly worried about competition from the young Englishman, who put in an eye-catching performance in one of van Persie's favoured positions out on the left.

He had cut a frustrated figure when he eventually did

come off the bench but van Persie told the *Daily Express* it only reflected his committed attitude. If he was not getting involved or he felt something was not right, van Persie was bound to make his feelings known.

He said: 'I'm not a guy who takes things easily in games. I always ask everything of myself – and, if things aren't going as they're supposed to, I get very disappointed. That's when I have to hold my temper. That's when I have to freeze it for a few moments. This is the best way for me to get the best out of myself.'

That uncompromising attitude had earned him that hothead reputation but as the years progressed he was learning to take a step back and control that temper. It would always be difficult for a player who was well known for having such a short fuse because he would forever be tested by opponents like Jimmy-Floyd Hasselbaink.

Arsenal were used to the velvety surface of the Emirates and it was a nasty shock for the team when they travelled to CSKA Moscow in the Champions League. The Gunners went down 1-0 in the freezing conditions as the pitch completely messed up a van Persie chance. It compared to that difficult League Cup night he had pulled through at Doncaster's old Belle Vue stadium. Van Persie sprinted clear and a goal looked certain before the ball bobbled horribly off the turf and his momentum was taken away. Thierry Henry was livid when van Persie was through again but got caught in possession when he should really have squared to the Frenchman.

Henry lost his temper and ranted at van Persie as he felt the Dutchman wasted a perfect goalscoring opportunity. Arsène Wenger did his best to play down talk of a rift between the two strikers and said it was only natural for players to get annoyed every now and again. He said: 'Strikers always get frustrated but I don't see any problem with them. Robin has improved tremendously. When he came here he was not in the team at Feyenoord, and is now a regular in the Dutch national team. That tells you the strides he has made and I think he is a great player. He got frustrated on one occasion on Tuesday. He showed hesitation, touched the ball again and then it was too late as the keeper had come out. But that can happen.'

It seemed peculiar that van Persie could play so well for his country but had only scored three times for his club after nearly three months of the season. Henry was one of the greatest players in the world and would become angry when other players were not quite up to his unparalleled abilities. He would have to learn to be patient with van Persie though because the Dutchman was still trying to find that consistency so desperately needed to help him make the step up.

A great big bowl of sour grapes was the order of the day from Chelsea manager José Mourinho who was incensed to see his side's players booked for leaving the pitch to celebrate goals with supporters. He pointed out that van Persie had not been shown a card after the goal at Charlton despite leaving the pitch, hurdling advertising hoardings and climbing a set of stairs to embrace fans. It did seem bizarre that the same referee would go on to book the Chelsea players and it highlighted one of the inconsistencies in the modern game.

Van Persie was back to scoring ways when Arsenal travelled to Reading. A well-crafted team move involving

Alexander Hleb and van Persie's best mate Thierry Henry saw the Dutchman casually sweep the ball home in a 4-0 win. The number 11 was back to something like his best and had supporters foaming at the mouth when he set off on an incredible 60-yard run before flashing past a post. It would have been even better than that wonder goal at The Valley. Those old disciplinary problems returned when van Persie smashed into goalkeeper Marcus Hahnemann when trying to follow up a Fàbregas shot. He was extremely lucky to escape with just a word in the ear from referee Alan Wiley.

Henry said it had been a good team victory and he was right because not only were the players on song, they were combining brilliantly and Reading were not able to cope. When Everton visited the Emirates, van Persie produced another of those magical free-kicks. There were a completely unnecessary four players over the ball and they stood still as van Persie ran up, checked his run and ran again before curling the ball over the Toffees' wall and towards the top right-hand corner of the goal. Tim Howard was across his goal well enough to get a hand on the shot but there was too much power behind it and he could only deflect it into the back of the net.

It was another beautiful strike from van Persie and the Arsenal commercial team must have been rubbing their hands with glee at the prospect of a top-selling end of season DVD. As he celebrated another classic goal, Bouchra would have been glad to read reports her husband had been seen ignoring the advances of several girls on a night at London's famous Chinawhite nightclub that weekend.

CSKA Moscow again frustrated Arsenal in the return fixture at the Emirates as van Persie was one of the Gunners players guilty of missing golden opportunities from close range during a Cold War style affair. It could have been a very different evening had van Persie not screwed a close-range effort over the bar with five minutes gone. He also flashed a header just wide of the far post and Henry could not understand how his side had failed to score. Van Persie had not been the only one to spurn a great opportunity as the side just could not put the chances away. He said: 'We had the right aggressiveness, the right attitude and played good football. We created chances once again and did not put the ball in the back of the net... Cesc had one, Robin van Persie had three. We had so many opportunities.'

After the game, a very frank van Persie admitted his distribution and passing had to improve if he was to become a better player. He told the *Evening Standard*: 'I want to help my team mates, I want them to trust me in every situation and know that I am there to help on the pitch. It is important for a striker to work hard for the team. That can be through goals, assists or just being there for your colleagues.'

That old message of playing as a team was back with a vengeance and van Persie was sure a more united Arsenal would be able to pick up the slack. Maybe a more unselfish attitude would have already seen the side progress from their group in the Champions League; van Persie and Cesc Fàbregas were both heavily criticised for trying to go it alone too often.

The poor patch continued when van Persie fluffed his lines once more in a pathetic 1-0 defeat at West Ham. The Dutchman could have opened the scoring early on when set up by a Henry header but home keeper Robert Green was smartly down to tip the ball around the post. Once again van

Persie's temper frayed and he was booked for a rash sliding tackle after having been roughed up by Jonathan Spector.

The Upton Park fans were less than impressed with his bullish attitude and he was struck by a coin thrown from the stands. It was Hamburg away all over again as 'flash' van Persie was barracked by fans all afternoon long before being substituted to a chorus of boos in the second half. It was a strange decision to pull the star off because he had been the Arsenal player who had posed the most consistent threat on the home goal – Van Persie thrived in situations like this after being brought up in the hostile environments of heated derbies back in the Netherlands.

It was often the skilful players who were targeted by home fans, and with him also having been accused of rape, some opposition supporters would see van Persie as an obvious choice when looking for somebody at whom to vent their frustrations. He fell to the floor after being struck by the two-pence coin and the hostile atmosphere only got worse from then onwards. Play was halted for several minutes whilst van Persie received treatment and police officers searched for the coin on the floor.

After the game, West Ham manager Alan Pardew rightly commented that there was no place for this kind of incident in football and that he hoped the offender could be traced from CCTV camera footage. Fortunately for Arsenal, rather than being knocked back by such an incident, it would only serve to spur van Persie on and make him more determined.

The Football Association vowed to launch a thorough investigation after the game in order to make sure the offender was suitably punished. Somewhat predictably, however, footage was not able to help identify the culprit and no charges were ever made.

Former England manager Graham Taylor told the *Daily Telegraph* that van Persie was one of the best young talents around in the Premier League and that he was sure those recent poor performances would soon be left in the past.

Ahead of Arsenal's clash with Liverpool, the Merseysiders' Dirk Kuyt said he was desperate to get one over on his international team mate van Persie. Kuyt said the move to England had seen van Persie grow up quickly as he become increasingly involved in the side. He said: 'He is growing a lot as a player and as a man. It is great to see him doing so well there.'

After that Hamburg flash point van Persie had insisted he was not a cheat but actions prove louder than words and he badly let himself down with a deliberate handball during the convincing 3-0 win over Kuyt's team. When he was bearing down on Pepe Reina's goal, van Persie saw fit to punch the ball past the Spanish goalkeeper before rolling the ball into the unguarded net. He then had the nerve to run off in celebration before being brought back down to earth with a much-deserved yellow card from his old friend referee Mark Clattenburg. It was completely farcical for van Persie to think he could get away with such blatant foul play – who did he think he was, Diego Maradona? After the game he insisted he was not a cheater but that he always had winning on his mind.

On 16 November 2006, his wife Bouchra gave birth to the couple's first child, a boy named Shaqueel. Robin was very proud they had brought a new life into the world. He would later tell the Netherlands World Cup Blog that having a child completely changed the couple's life. Robin said: 'He's my everything. Every day is an adventure – for him and for us and it changed us. My wife and I lived a bohemian life before. Now, we are very responsible. Maybe even too much. I never used my seatbelt for instance. Now, it's the first thing I strap on in the car. I don't speed anymore. My wife even loves me more now she sees me as a dad. Gilberto once said to me that motherhood is the toughest job in the world. And it is. Twenty-four hours on call. I admire her.'

The arrival of Shaqueel meant van Persie was to miss the friendly meeting between the Netherlands and England. This might have been a blessing in disguise as he had an opportunity to rest after a hectic last few weeks.

With the news of his fatherhood reigniting talk about van Persie back home in the Netherlands, newspapers began saying he was the new Johan Cruyff. He would have to put up with comparisons to Cruyff and Bergkamp for the whole of his career but van Persie was now a down-to-earth player who was able to take newspaper speculation with a pinch of salt. After all, he had been stung by the press in the past, so was not terribly interested in what they were saying. He said: 'Yes, it's flattering but I try not to think about it. I try to give it my best shot every time I'm on the field. It's kind of people to say nice things but I don't think "Oh my God they think I'm the next Cruyff." I know that a month later the same people might be hammering me. That's how life is at the top in football.'

The way things had gone so far in van Persie's career, he was cruising for a bruising. Newcastle United's no-nonsense midfielder Nicky Butt gave him just that with a crunching tackle that left van Persie badly limping. He had to be replaced at half-time with Arsène Wenger looking deeply concerned afterwards and saying he did not think van Persie's foot was looking good. Fortunately he was able to train just days later and a club statement said the injury was not as serious as had first been feared.

He played an important part as Arsenal beat Hamburg 3-1 to qualify for the knockout stages of the Champions League. The Germans had been on top and took an early lead before van Persie sparked a change in fortune with an important goal. Cesc Fàbregas put him through with a defence-splitting ball and van Persie steadied himself before firing in at the near post. As Fàbregas' pass came to van Persie from his left-hand side, it fell more comfortably to his right foot and he confidently prodded home without making it obvious that it was very much his weaker foot.

He went close with a spectacular free-kick and also had an effort hacked off the line as Arsenal motored back to top the group. Van Persie had been pushed further forward in the second half and the side's more direct approach was rewarded when the goals eventually came. Wenger labelled it a convincing comeback and praised the tenacity of a side that refused to feel sorry for itself.

As they got stuck back into some Premier League action at Craven Cottage, Antti Niemi became the latest goalkeeper to be beaten by a van Persie free-kick. He was a good 30 yards from goal and not exactly central, but once that left foot had been wrapped around the ball the Finland goalkeeper had no chance as the ball curled into the top left-hand corner of the goal. It was not enough for Arsenal as they slipped to a 2-1 defeat against dark horses Fulham and started to lose touch with the top of the table – now a massive 16 points behind Manchester United. Arsène Wenger had all but thrown in the towel, with Arsenal way off the pace.

Former Arsenal manager George Graham chipped in with an observation that van Persie had not filled the hole left by Bergkamp because he was more of an out-and-out striker than his countryman, who was more involved in their link play. The freedom allowed to van Persie had worked wonders for the Netherlands team but Graham was not sure that approach was right for Arsenal. He said: 'He [Wenger] has spent money on players like Tomáš Rosický, Alexander Hleb and Robin van Persie, and I don't really know where any of them play. They are all very comfortable on the ball and are good passers, but they drift all over the place.'

The Gunners relieved some of that pain with a 3-0 win over Tottenham – just what the doctor had ordered. Gilberto Silva twice dispatched penalties after van Persie had been fouled. However there was a fresh blot on van Persie's name when he handled on the way to winning the second penalty. Had he suddenly got the idea that it would be all right to use his hands?

Van Persie looked out of sorts as Arsenal grabbed a credible draw at second-placed Chelsea. It was another of those off-days that he had said were going to become a thing of the past back in the summer. He hit a free-kick into the wall and later shot well wide of the target before putting a free header over the bar. Wenger benched him for the next league game as Emmanuel Adebayor had hit a purple patch.

The Togo striker was starting to limit van Persie's chances of making the first team and, unlike van Persie, he was able to beat David James when Portsmouth came to town. James performed heroics with an instinctively stuck-out leg blocking van Persie's downward header before later smothering at the striker's feet when he looked a certainty to score. And with the Gunners stumbling their way to a 2-2 draw, van Persie's last-minute decision to shoot from the left-hand touchline rather than pass to colleagues would have done him no favours whatsoever.

He was back on song next week against Blackburn and it was no coincidence that Arsenal ran out 6-2 winners. Van Persie set up Gilberto Silva to head home with an inch-perfect corner kick delivery that came straight from the training ground. Next van Persie got in on the action himself by cutting in from the right-hand flank to curl a left-footed shot into the far corner. Just minutes later he was perfectly slipped in for a beautiful second. After holding his run to perfection to beat the offside trap, he drove the ball home first time with his left foot, no questions asked. Wenger was thrilled with his second because it was the result of a magnificent collaboration between the forwards. He said it was a real Arsenal goal and the result of great collective play.

For Arsenal's third goal van Persie went down extremely easily under Lucas Neill's challenge to win a penalty that Adebayor punted in. He had technically been clipped by the Aussie but to exaggerate the contact was certainly under-hand from van Persie and this was not the kind of beautiful football Arsène Wenger would have wanted his team to play.

After the game van Persie insisted that there was no

better footballing side in the Premier League than Arsenal. He boasted: 'It is frustrating, but I see it in a positive way. We are proving every week that we are the best. I watch a lot of football and sometimes I see games on TV and I think "I could never play in that team." When I see those games, I am just happy I am in a team which plays fantastic football.'

Unfortunately for Arsenal, wins were awarded to the team who had put the ball in the opposition's net the most times and there was no reward for playing attractive football. With Arsenal still 14 points behind Manchester United, surely something didn't quite add up. Nevertheless, the future certainly looked bright for van Persie and he would have been licking his lips as Arsenal were drawn against PSV Eindhoven in the knockout stages of the Champions League.

It was the Dutch way to speak your mind and worry about making enemies later and van Persie went about making no friends whatsoever ahead of the Champions League meeting with PSV Eindhoven. He set up another of his infamous controversial spats when he claimed the Premier League was better than the Eredivisie and he knew the weaknesses of every member of the squad. He could not help himself when given the chance to talk down the club that had been a fierce rival in his Feyenoord days, even though he risked firing up the opponents in the process.

He made it 10 goals for the season with a timely winner in the 2-1 triumph at Watford. Theo Walcott threaded through to the Dutchman and he cut inside at pace before curling the ball into the bottom corner to seal the three points. It had not gone unnoticed that van Persie had weighed in with his fair share of assists this season and Wenger praised the way he had been setting up team mates instead of just shooting at the first sight of goal.

Wenger said van Persie had been a lot more grown up this season and highlighted his importance to the team, enthusing: 'There is some Bergkamp in him, in the way he finishes, his quick decisions and the way he strikes the ball cleanly. His goal was a great finish and now he is maturing and developing into a team player.'

Despite stepping in with some important goals in the past few weeks, van Persie said his side was missing Thierry Henry, who had been out for a number of weeks. He added: 'But even without him we are doing quite well and that is a big compliment for ourselves at the moment.'

He had certainly bulked up and toughened up since joining the Gunners but van Persie was given a rough ride as his side crashed to a disastrous defeat to Sheffield United at Bramall Lane. The side had just come up from the Championship and gave Arsenal's pampered stars a glimpse of what things were like further down the English football pyramid.

Arsène Wenger complained afterwards that the Yorkshire side had targeted van Persie unfairly and that some of the challenges made had been 'hard to take'. There was even an allegation he had been punched by the Blades' skipper Chris Morgan. He wailed: 'What is physical? Is a punch in the stomach physical? I feel for a long time there is a misunderstanding between me and the press about what is physical.' Morgan was charged with misconduct by the FA in the new year.

To rub salt into van Persie's wounds, he was denied a last-minute equaliser when defender Phil Jagielka, who had taken over in goal from the injured Paddy Kenny, pulled off an incredible full-length diving save. Jagielka later branded Arsenal 'big babies' after they had moaned their way through the 90 minutes and van Persie had even refused to shake Keith Gillespie's hand at the final whistle, pushing the Northern Ireland man out of his way.

It was an unfortunate way to end the year but his national coach Marco van Basten said van Persie had been the best young European player in the international game in the past year and backed him for more of the same in 2007. He said van Persie was developing wonderfully under his ally Arsène Wenger and that despite his side's gutless exit to Portugal, van Persie had been very impressive at the World Cup and was sure to go on to bigger and better things in the new year.

Van Basten told the *Sunday Mirror*: 'He has so much natural talent. Before the World Cup I had a different idea about the strongest and most experienced team for Holland. Robin was not an established player yet, but when he arrived in the training camp he was unbelievably fit and so full of energy.'

The former World and European Player of the Year admitted he had completely changed his tactics in order to include van Persie in the side after he had shone so brightly in training. Van Persie was extremely fortunate that his national coach had such an open mind because a lot of managers adopt a very set idea about how their team should line up and are rarely swayed from that.

Van Persie responded by saying that without Wenger and van Basten in his life, he would have remained very much an individual and would not have learned to operate as part of a team: 'Before I had met Arsène Wenger and Marco van Basten I was an individual. I was aware I had been blessed with some talent, I used to do some tricks on a football pitch, but that was it. In really big matches I did not know what to do when there was no time or space for tricks and skills.

'At Arsenal and with van Basten I learned to play fast and simple, I got good lessons in fast combination football. I started to make big runs for other strikers and create space for our midfielders. Coming to Arsenal and working with van Basten are the two most important things in my career.'

That had been evident in the first half of the 2006/07 season as van Persie became a lot more involved in build-up play for Arsenal. For the Netherlands he had learned to focus his attentions to setting up chances for centre forward van Nistelrooy from the right flank and as a result became a better team player for his club.

That team spirit shone through when van Persie scored two goals in a centre forward role as Arsenal got their year off to a bang with a 4-0 humbling of Charlton. That made it five goals in four matches for van Persie and the Addicks must have been glad to see the back of their Dutch nemesis.

Thierry Henry marked his return to the side by opening the scoring with a penalty that was won by van Persie. Charlton defender Osei Sankofa could not deal with van Persie's pace, panicked and dragged him down for a red card. Charlton boss Alan Pardew later claimed van Persie had gone down 'quite dramatically'. Van Persie scored a later penalty himself before rounding things off with another strike in the last minute to take his tally to 12 for the season.

Henry said everybody knew that van Persie could score

goals from the centre forward position and that he was irresistible in his current form. He had done his best to keep that great scoring run going for his team mate when he unselfishly allowed him to take that second penalty. Henry had been the player fouled in the lead up to the spot kick but he said he was willing to pass up a chance to a team mate and was 'not obsessed with goals'.

He added that van Persie had the potential to become one of the greatest players in the history of the Premier League: 'If he wants it and if his head is right, like it is at the moment, he can be, in years to come, one of the best ever in the Premiership. It would be great if he finished as Arsenal's top scorer. That would be something special for him. Robin is doing it for the national team and is doing it for Arsenal. It is up to him how far he is going to go.'

Henry challenged van Persie to see how far he could go in the game and insisted he had to be his own man. That was a view shared by van Persie as he looked to make the number 11 shirt his own and leave Bergkamp's hallowed number 10 alone for now.

Normality was restored in the 3-1 FA Cup win at Liverpool when Henry resumed goalscoring responsibilities and van Persie dropped back to play in the supporting role he had taken to so well before Henry's injury. Van Persie nearly netted a goal of his own but was denied by Jerzy Dudek after doing well to find the target with his right foot. The pair combined brilliantly throughout and van Persie also went close after Henry's clever clipped pass, but Jamie Carragher made an impressive last-ditch tackle. It was the perfect set-up for Henry as he finally had a strike partner with whom he was able to form an understanding.

With the return of Henry to the side, van Persie's goals had started to dry up. He had only just got used to being the team's focal point and leading goal threat so it must have been a shock to the system to be bumped back down once King Thierry came back from injury. Their 2-0 win at Blackburn a few days later saw things continue in a similar vein, with Henry scoring and taking the plaudits whilst van Persie did his best to create chances and bring the ball forward.

Not scoring did not make him a bad player but it must have been frustrating as Henry marched straight back into the side and picked up where he left off. Lucas Neill renewed acquaintances with his old adversary by sticking to tradition and hacking van Persie down en route to goal. Van Persie did well not to lose his temper after receiving his regular slice of roughhousing.

His clash with Neill had softened up those notoriously delicate ankles and when he picked up another niggle in training, van Persie was a doubt for the clash with Manchester United. The one thing blocking his rise to stardom was his susceptibility to injury and although he was fit in time for the Emirates clash, he was soon wishing he had not been.

Coming off the bench, van Persie quickly made a big difference when he turned home a Fàbregas cross to draw Arsenal level in a game they would go on to win 2-1. Disastrously, in connection with the ball van Persie broke the fifth metatarsal in his right foot. An x-ray right after the game confirmed the injury and had Wenger deeply concerned. He said: 'There is a big worry on Robin van Persie. He had scored a great goal coming from a very deep position and scored an unbelievable effort, but he can deliver that.'

Wenger was scared that after doing so well without Henry and then linking up with the star excellently after his return, van Persie would be missing for a lengthy period of time. He was right because despite an initial diagnosis of two months' recovery time, this injury effectively wrote off the Dutchman's season. He was reduced to a watching brief as Arsenal crashed out of the Champions League against PSV, made little headway in the domestic cups and were beaten to third place in the Premier League on goal difference by Liverpool. It was a poor end to the season, but despite being out for a large chunk of it, Robin van Persie was Arsenal's leading goalscorer with 13 in all competitions.

CHAPTER SIX

NEW RESPONSIBILITIES

With Thierry Henry leaving Arsenal for Barcelona in the summer, it was down to van Persie to take greater goalscoring responsibility in the 2007/08 season. He had been near fitness at the end of the previous season but Wenger had decided that it was not worth risking further injury with Arsenal having nothing left to play for in what had been a disappointing season for the team.

Van Persie was in amongst the goals in pre-season and ready to lead the line for an Arsenal side that had once again been shorn of one of its big-name players in post-season. In another quiet comeback game, he slid in at the far post to score against Turkish outfit Gençlerbirliği, an extremely similar effort to the one he hit against United which led to his injury. This time he had not broken anything when scoring the goal and it was time to crack on with the new season. He told the *Evening Standard*: 'For me it is like, "Okay, I scored that goal against United and I

163

scored a similar goal now." So that is it. This period has gone. It is time to get it on and start again. It is in the past, it is history.'

Wenger had protected van Persie from meeting old foes Ajax in the past but this pre-season he decided not to wrap his lead marksman in cotton wool. The Dutch side decided it would be appropriate to kick the former Feyenoord man around the park in this 'friendly' but it looked like van Persie had got the last laugh when he prodded home the winner with minutes to go.

Perhaps in hindsight this had not been the wisest of times and places to score a goal and within seconds he had been flattened by John Heitinga. Wenger would have been ruing his decision to play van Persie had he been seriously injured. He retained a stiff upper lip after the game and reasoned that his side had faced similar tactics from the likes of Sheffield United and Doncaster Rovers before. He said: 'The idea that you have to kick Arsenal is well known in England and it has obviously travelled over the border. It doesn't worry me that teams might try to kick us because the best response is to win.'

Clearly the streets of Amsterdam were never going to be a safe place for van Persie to roam, but he had shown that he would not be stopped and would not be riled and had been rewarded with the winning goal. Emerging from that game with a goal and without having been provoked into a red card was a real triumph for van Persie.

Ahead of the season Arsenal were labelled good but not quite experienced enough by a lot of pundits including former Spurs and England man Les Ferdinand. The legendary striker did tell the *Guardian* he thought van

Persie was 'decent', which, coming from a former Tottenham player, was praise indeed.

Arsène Wenger was starting to run out of strikers so it was important the ones he did have at his disposal were able to play together. He said van Persie had the potential to link up well with Adebayor, who contrasted with the Dutchman well because whilst he provided a little less skill, the Togo man was a powerhouse who would bully defences and give the front line a little more bite. Wenger said: 'I think he is developing very, very well. He has become more mature and he benefits from the good work of Emmanuel Adebayor, who makes room for him. The two always combine well together.'

Giovanni van Bronckhorst had done the opposite to van Persie and moved from Arsenal to Feyenoord in the summer. After leaving he said van Persie had made immeasurable progress since first breaking onto the scene and he believed van Persie was ready to step up and become an even more important player for club and country. He told the *Guardian*: 'If you compare him now to the boy who made his debut for the Dutch team – I remember him as a wiry, self-confident kid – his development has been tremendous. He's more consistent now and stronger. He's ready to take over a role as a leader in the team, both at Arsenal and with Holland, and Dutch fans recognise him as a star player for the future of the national team.'

As had been expected, van Persie started the season as the focal point of the Arsenal attack and things started well as he netted a penalty in a 2-1 win over Fulham. He could have had a couple more but that old foe, the woodwork, denied him further goals. It was hardly a vintage performance but at least this season had actually started with a win. Fulham manager Lawrie Sanchez had accused van Persie of taking a dive during the game but later apologised after having seen the incidents again on television.

Van Persie was on similar white-hot form in a 2-0 Champions League qualifying victory at Sparta Prague. He was incredibly unfortunate not to get on the score sheet after twice being denied by goalkeeper Tomas Postulka. First the stopper beat his free-kick away from danger before diving brilliantly to tip a low drive around the post after van Persie had tricked his way into the box with a smart dummy.

He was also booked in that game after giving as good as he got from the pushy Czechs. Wenger was thrilled to see his side standing up for themselves and told the *Evening Standard*: 'You have got a team like this, and maybe they think this is the way to play against Arsenal. However, we have to show we are not the same team as before and are ready for the challenge.'

Van Persie scored his second goal in as many league games in the bad-tempered 1-1 draw with Blackburn Rovers. The goal showed how far van Persie had come in developing his game as it was a real striker's finish to take advantage of a defensive mix-up and prod home the ball as it bounced around the penalty area.

The commentary team on *Match of the Day* were very excited by van Persie's solo effort: 'You'd have to travel a long, long way to see a better goal than that. Absolutely stunning. The surge of pace, the close control, the balance, the finish. Bergkamp may be in the twilight of his career but there's another Dutchman very much in the springtime of his.'

Wenger claimed Blackburn had a 'desire for violence' but Blackburn manager Mark Hughes angrily responded that it had been van Persie who had committed the worst foul of the game. He did however have the grace to admit that van Persie had tormented Blackburn for a number of seasons and was destined to become the club's main man. He told the *Sunday Express*: 'Van Persie has been a thorn in our side in recent years, he is an outstanding talent and maybe it's time for him to step up to the mark and be the main man.'

One of the things a main man should be able to do is step up, take a penalty and score. Van Persie let his team down at Manchester City when his spot kick was too close to goalkeeper Kasper Schmeichel and the Dane knocked away with his feet. Schmeichel's father, the Manchester United legend Peter, had saved a spot kick from Dennis Bergkamp in 1999 and Wenger quipped that he hoped he wouldn't have to come up against Peter's grandson in a few years' time. Cesc Fàbregas spared van Persie's blushes when he scored the winner but this was still highly embarrassing for van Persie.

Adebayor came out in his team mate's defence and said everybody knew van Persie was still a top-class player. He rejected any suggestions somebody else should be given penalty-kick taking duties and said the team had every confidence in the Dutchman. He pleaded to be given time to forge a partnership with van Persie, with whom he already enjoyed a good relationship away from the field.

Arsenal had been kicked around the pitch by Ajax and Blackburn already this season and van Persie was still seething about that rough treatment after the Manchester City game. He told the *Sunday Times* that kind of tactic had nothing to do with football; it was all about teams stopping Arsenal from playing their game properly. Pundits on *Match of the Day* had mocked Wenger for complaining his players were being targeted and van Persie was not amused. He said: 'I think the boss has the right to tell the cameras about it, to say something to the people back home. It's not honest to say, "Arsenal is always moaning".'

Blackburn loudmouth midfielder Robbie Savage later hit back when he called van Persie a hypocrite and claimed Arsenal gave as good as they got. He said that because Arsenal were a big London club, people would only write positive things about them.

They were presenting a more aggressive front since the Blackburn game and van Persie made his presence felt during the 3-0 second-leg stroll to victory over Sparta Prague. Van Persie was having none of the nonsense Tomas Repka had tried in the away game and hauled the former West Ham bully to the ground by his neck in a feisty opening.

A few days later it was van Persie's time to hit the deck as Portsmouth goalkeeper David James sent him sprawling. Despite Adebayor's support for the Dutchman after that penalty was saved in Manchester, it was the Togo man who stood up to rifle home the penalty in a 3-1 win. Arsenal were going well but van Persie was not as involved as he would have liked as they beat Spurs at White Hart Lane to go top of the Premier League.

A second half strike in a 3-0 Champions League win over Sevilla proved the perfect medicine and van Persie purred that Arsenal had were playing 'football from a different world' after the game. His goal came after Bacary Sagna flicked on to the far post and van Persie smashed the ball home from close range.

Van Persie was thrilled with the spirit showed by the squad in the win after they had looked a bit off the boil at the end of last season. He told the *Evening Standard* it was all down to Arsène Wenger insisting the team could achieve so much more if they worked as a unit. He said: 'He brought this learning to everyone. I know everyone is thinking the Arsenal way and that can make a big difference. Not many teams play the way we play.' The Gunners had won seven of their first eight games of the season so it was little wonder van Persie was so pleased with the way things were going.

Wenger said his side had played through the 'pain barrier' of matches like the Blackburn one and were now reaping the rewards of their new steely resolve.

As September drew to an end, van Persie netted his fourth of the season at West Ham to open up a three-point lead at the top of the table. A perfect Alexander Hleb cross was nodded goalwards by van Persie and although Robert Green got a hand to it, the effort had too much power behind it and ended up in the back of the net via a post. It was rare for him to score a header but it was clear van Persie was doing all he could to lead the Gunners' title charge.

The Premier League seemed to have a bit more bite to it than in previous years and nothing will have said 'welcome to Upton Park' quite like Lee Bowyer's harsh early hack at van Persie. The Arsenal players had probably packed their helmets but there were no coins thrown from the stands this time around. Wenger was again critical of the rough treatment his players had been given, but surely by going on these rants he was only giving out signals that rough tactics did affect his players.

Back in European action, van Persie scored the only goal as Arsenal secured their ninth straight win with a 1-0 success at Steaua Bucharest. He was in the right place at the right time to slot home from an Adebayor cutback. Van Persie said Arsenal were playing a special and unique brand of football and praised Arsène Wenger for not rotating the squad too much, as certain other Premier League bosses had a knack of doing.

Van Persie was in a rich vein of form and scored an impressive brace in a nail-biting 3-2 win over Sunderland. He rocketed yet another unstoppable free-kick past Craig Gordon and remained a threat for the rest of the afternoon before smacking home from close range at the death to seal the win.

That great run had to come to an end sooner or later and once again van Persie picked up a knock, this time whilst on international duty. He had set up a goal in a 2-0 qualifying victory over Slovenia but later took a knock to his knee and faced a month on the sidelines. Wenger was understandably upset at losing the striker to injury once again and told Arsenal TV: 'It is a big blow. Robin is a striker, a supportive striker and important on set-pieces as well. I hope he will be back soon and we'll do the maximum to get him back.'

It was a longer lay-off than expected and he did not make a comeback until the New Year after suffering muscular injuries alongside the existing knee problem. He made a surprise comeback as Arsenal drew 1-1 with Tottenham in the League Cup semi-final but had to be withdrawn at half-time as something was clearly not right, with the Dutchman well off the pace. He did not feature again until coming off the bench in a 0-0 draw at Wigan Athletic, with Arsenal having maintained their position at the top of the Premier League in his absence. Lacking a bit of match sharpness, van Persie wastefully blasted a free-kick well over the bar where he might usually have worried the goalkeeper.

Finally he was ready to start as Middlesbrough visited the Emirates in mid-March. He fired an early warning shot with an effort that went just wide in the first five minutes but again offered little else and was withdrawn on the hour mark. This was an incredibly frustrating period after all the hype about it being his biggest Arsenal season and he had once again gone missing midway through a season. How was Arsène Wenger supposed to be able to count on him to be Arsenal's top striker if he only played in about half the team's games?

He told Arsenal TV that he had started the season with some very big ideas and ambition and that had not been messed up by this latest setback. The injuries had not beaten van Persie and he vowed to end the season strongly with Arsenal after saying he felt the side were a little unlucky not to be top of the table.

Van Persie was determined his side would pick up a trophy at the end of the season to make sure all their hard work had not been for nothing. It had been a frustrating injury-plagued period for him but unlike last season, Arsenal were still very much in with a shot at the Premier League title as well as having a Champions League quarter-final against Liverpool to look forward to.

Van Persie told the *Daily Star* he believed the team had the ability to take the Double of Premier League and Champions League and that now was their moment. He said: 'We have something here. We can win the Double but belief is 50 per cent of it. I still think we can do it, and hopefully I can play a part in it. I'm not a daydreamer, I really think we can win the title and the Champions League this season. Why not? We have the quality and the belief which can take you very far.'

Arsenal's title chances took a huge blow as they went down to two late Didier Drogba goals at Stamford Bridge. Carlo Cudicini had been inspired in the Chelsea goal and made two tremendous saves to keep van Persie from scoring. They bounced back from this defeat – and 2-0 down at Bolton – with three second-half goals at the Reebok. Van Persie had been a threat with several long-distance attempts going close and he hit his first goal in nearly six months when he rammed home a penalty.

Arsenal faced a triple header against Liverpool as the sides' league meeting was sandwiched in between both legs of that quarter-final. Before the game Dirk Kuyt told the *Liverpool Daily Echo* his international team mate would be the man to watch in the meetings. He said: 'Van Persie is a very good player. For me, he is the best Dutch player around at the moment, so we will have to be careful with him. He scored a good goal at the weekend so he will be feeling confident and keen to do well after being out injured for so long.'

As the sides drew the first leg of the Champions League game 1-1 at the Emirates, van Persie could only manage 45 minutes as he again left the field early with a recurrence of that thigh problem. That forced him out of the league game, which ended with the same score line, and he could only come on as an ineffective substitute in the 4-2 second leg exit at Anfield.

Arsenal would now have to concentrate on the Premier League and there was no time to rest as they travelled to Old Trafford just five days later in what was sure to be the title decider. Van Persie got the evening off to a flier when he crossed for Adebayor to bundle home the opening goal. It was a cheeky contribution from the Dutchman after he had taken a short free-kick and skipped round the side of the United defence before setting up the opener in sensational style. Cristiano Ronaldo and Owen Hargreaves hit back as United ran out 2-1 winners and effectively ended Arsenal's title push.

Arsenal won their last four games but it was too little, too late as Manchester United won the league, with Chelsea two points behind and the Gunners in third. If they had won at Old Trafford, Wenger's men would have won the league.

The manager knew van Persie could have contributed so much more if only he had remained free of injury. Arsenal had failed to win a trophy for the third season running but Wenger was confident van Persie would return from Euro 2008 to be a driving force for Arsenal. He said: 'Robin is unfortunate with injuries at the moment but in my opinion it is nothing more than that. He has so much talent so I am very keen to keep him, I trust him and I hope that he will get rid of his injuries. For me, Robin van Persie is a world-class footballer and you always hope that next season Robin will have an injury-free season.'

The season had ended in disappointment once again for van Persie but he dusted himself down and was desperate to do well for the Netherlands at Euro 2008 in Austria and Switzerland. It was going to be tough as he had not had a decent run in the Arsenal team since the tail end of the previous year and van Persie admitted before the tournament started that if he was able to play in the tournament, he would certainly not be firing on all cylinders.

Coach Marco van Basten put his crocked star on a special preparation programme as he trained separately from the rest of the squad, working with a physiotherapist to avoid further aggravating the niggles from which he was recovering.

The coach was being extremely accommodating to van Persie; maybe van Basten saw a little of himself in the Arsenal man because he had suffered from his own injury problems throughout his playing career. Van Persie admitted it was very draining as he tried his best to come back from the problems in time for the first game. He said: 'It is tiring both physically and psychologically because each time I thought I was getting back to being fully fit, I had a reverse. The coach has confidence in me, which is very pleasing and reassuring.'

Van Basten said he did not mind if van Persie missed the first match because he was a special player and worth the patience that was being shown in him. And how did van Persie repay van Basten for making an exception to many rules to allow him a shot of making the opening game?

Robin van Persie decided it would be a good idea to fall out with Wesley Sneijder and go into a reckless tackle on his team mate. The pair had apparently fallen out and had not been on speaking terms for a while but for things to erupt in the way they did would not have done the nation any favours ahead of their opening game. It looked like another rift would tear apart the side – reminiscent of the 1996 European Championships tournament when battling midfielder Edgar Davids was sent home after an argument.

After a precautionary visit to hospital it emerged that Real Madrid man Sneijder would be fit to start the mouthwatering opening game against Italy, but that van Persie would not.

The Netherlands produced a stunning 3-0 win to shock the reigning world champions, with van Persie making a cheeky 20-minute appearance after being brought on from the bench. It was a wonderful performance full of pace and attacking intent that reminded van Persie of the way his Arsenal side had gone about their business that season. He said: 'We want to show you can win a big title playing great football – it's what we believe in. We played some wonderful football against the world champions.'

For all the glory, there were still signs that all was not well in the Dutch camp as an angry Sneijder barked orders at his team mates for the entirety of the game and most of them chose to ignore him for the 90 minutes.

The Dutch did even better in their next match as they beat World Cup 2006 finalists France 4-1 in Bern. Both van Persie and his rival Sneijder hit the back of the net after van Persie was once again brought on from the bench. Van Persie had only been on the field for four minutes when Arjen Robben sent an inviting ball across the face of the goal and van Persie motored in at the back stick to sweep home.

Marco van Basten said it was brilliant to have van Persie available to come on during the game and pose a real threat. He said: 'We needed more players to stretch France and in bringing on Robin van Persie and Arjen Robben for the second half, we had more chances to go deep and that helped us and gave us more space. With these players, it is difficult for our opponents. They are quick and technical so we were much more dangerous in the second half.'

The Dutch had already qualified from the tournament's 'group of death' with a match to spare but there was to be no let-up in that final game against Romania. Van Persie was poised for his first start of the finals and was determined it would be another victory for his team. He joked that he did not even like to lose a game of table tennis in his house let alone a match at a World Cup finals, so Romania must have known they were in for a tough match.

Van Persie notched his second of the tournament as a second-string Dutch side strolled to a 2-0 win. As the game drew to a close he showed great focus to chest down a pass, make progress towards the goal and wallop a left-footed volley into the back of the net. The assembled Orange army went ballistic after seeing their heroes take maximum points from three hugely impressive displays.

After that win van Persie insisted that it had not been a Netherlands 'B' team because the whole squad formed one team and all 23 players were equals. He added: 'With this squad I really have the feeling that we are unbeatable, though we have to take it step by step. That is why I just want to be part of the team as it feels like something beautiful is happening.'

Van Basten said the players had done well in all three games despite a range of personnel being used. Suddenly the Dutch were touted as one of the favourites to win the tournament and their record from the group stage spoke for itself: played three, won three, scored nine, conceded one. The striker had come so far in a matter of days; it had looked like he would play little to no part in the tournament whatsoever and then he scored two and put in a Man of the Match performance against Romania.

When the Netherlands came up against unfancied Russia in the quarter-finals, supporters must have presumed their side would stroll their way through to the semis. Guus Hiddink had other ideas and the Russians' Dutch coach watched his side lead for a long period through Roman Pavlyuchenko's goal just after the break. It was a big shock and only a last-minute Ruud van Nistelrooy effort kept the Dutch in the tournament.

Things went from bad to worse in extra time however, as the Russians hit two more goals without reply to power through to the semi-finals. The Dutch were shell-shocked to be out after such a rampant display in the group stages. Van Persie had warned at the start of the season that to be the best you needed to be able to deliver to a consistent level and his Dutch team had been unable to do that after having an off day at exactly the wrong time.

Marco van Basten said he did not understand how the side had played so badly after most of the team had been given the best part of a week to rest. The introduction of van Persie had been unable to change things and the Dutch were out. Van Basten said: 'In the second half we brought Robin van Persie in for a bit more depth, but the Russians played very well. In the group stage we played good football, but we didn't play to such a high level as that on Saturday.'

It was incomprehensible that this would happen after the Dutch had played so well in their first three games. Some supporters wondered if it had been wise for them to go all-out in that final game which had nothing riding on it.

Perhaps it was a case of 'too much too soon' for the Dutch and they should have saved some of their best play for later on in the tournament instead of burning themselves out at an early stage.

Arsenal had slowly been losing members of their squad as players like Mathieu Flamini were leaving on free transfers after the Gunners refused to meet their wage demands. Van Persie, who was in the initial stages of discussing a new deal for himself, said the side needed to be more flexible with wages offered if they wanted to attract top players to the Emirates and keep them there.

He said: 'Arsenal have a policy in which they will not go over a specific amount of money when agreeing the salary of a player. I think they should go to a higher level of salary. If you are 27 or 28 I can understand that you would make the decision to go elsewhere if you can earn three or four times as much.'

A couple of months after that disappointing European Championships exit, van Persie was back in an Arsenal shirt and looking every bit that improved player Wenger had prophesied he would return as. The season kicked off in the right way with van Persie setting up the opener in a 2-0 Champions League qualifying match against FC Twente. He might not have scored yet but his link-up play in the emphatic 4-0 second-leg win showed great promise for the coming season. Van Persie had insisted the Gunners 'needed' Champions League football and he had helped them secure a spot in the competition's group stages.

He was up and rolling for the season with a smart double against Newcastle at the Emirates. Van Persie shouldered penalty taking responsibilities when Charles N'Zogbia handled and perfectly hit his shot low and hard into the side netting to leave Shay Given no chance of making a save. The Republic of Ireland goalkeeper then worked wonders to keep out van Persie's free-kick before an Emmanuel Eboué backheel was prodded into the net by the Dutchman from close range. Van Persie was held in high esteem by the Arsenal faithful but the same could not be said for Emmanuel Adebayor who had expressed an interest in a move away from the club. When the Togo man came on in place of van Persie, there was a chorus of boos from the home crowd.

Van Persie would have relished making the trip to Ewood Park as he had always posed real problems for Blackburn in the past. Mark Hughes would have been having nightmares about van Persie but his side were not able to stop him from once again proving the thorn in Rovers' side. Van Persie allowed a Theo Walcott pass to roll across the front of his body before prodding past Paul Robinson. Van Persie later wastefully fired into the side netting before Adebayor excelled himself and hit a hat-trick.

Van Persie and Adebayor proved double trouble for Porto as both men netted braces in a 4-0 win in the opening Champions League group stage match. He had been somewhat patchy in the league but van Persie really found his stride against the Portuguese side. He opened the scoring after rushing to beat his man to the ball and sliding home from Adebayor's pass. He nutmegged poor Bruno Alves before slotting into the corner for his second goal of the evening. Wenger later said he had expected nothing less from the evening and that his side was showing big potential.

Another header in the home win against Everton set

Arsenal on their way to a 3-1 win to get back to winning ways after a far from perfect start to the season. Van Persie played his part in a scintillating North London derby when his 50th Arsenal goal looked to have finished off Spurs as Arsenal went 4-2 ahead. When van Persie began to tire and was replaced with 10 minutes left, the game was as good as won but somehow Spurs charged back and hit two goals to level the game. Arsène Wenger was fuming after the game that all Arsenal's hard work had been thrown away. There was nothing van Persie could do but watch from the bench as the side surrendered the lead.

It looked like van Persie had banished those old disciplinary problems to the past, but in a controversial defeat at Stoke City, he received a red card just 10 minutes after coming off the bench. It was a by-product of Stoke time-wasting after they had just gone 2-0 ahead. Andy Griffin headed back to Thomas Sorensen and the Denmark goalkeeper took his time in collecting the ball. Van Persie was in something of a rush and in no mood to allow the Potters players to run the clock down. As Sorensen bent down to collect the ball, van Persie barged into him in a vain attempt to win the ball. It was understandable that he also wanted to vent some frustration at play being held up. Sorensen fell to the floor in dramatic fashion and referee Rob Styles marched over brandishing a red card.

As he liked to do, Arsène Wenger defended his player to anybody who would listen once the final whistle had gone. He said the decision was extremely harsh on his star and ranted: 'If that's a red card I have to review my rule book.' Maybe it had been an unfair card but van Persie had still allowed himself to be wound up by the Stoke goalkeeper who would have known exactly what he was doing. The problem with making a name for yourself as a fiery character is that you might then be targeted by opposition players to see if they can get under your skin and force you to do something stupid. Wenger had hoped his man had grown out of that phase by now but there was evidently still a hot-headed lad inside that maturing body.

After serving a suspension van Persie had to endure a terrible comeback game as the Gunners were ripped to shreds in a 3-0 defeat at Manchester City. After wasting the opportunity to score from a free-kick, van Persie was muscled off the ball by Shaun Wright-Phillips in midfield and, quick as a flash, the Sky Blues had scored. Furthermore, he had not learned from that incident at the Britannia Stadium and decided it would be a good idea to take the ball from Joe Hart as he tried to take a goal kick. He was yellow carded as a result and was lucky to escape further action for this rash act.

He bounced back from that disaster brilliantly with one of the biggest performances of his Arsenal career so far, netting two quick-fire goals in a brilliant 2-1 win at Stamford Bridge to keep them in touch with leaders Liverpool. Just before the hour mark, van Persie was fed by Denilson and, ignoring calls of offside, smacked the ball home. His second was a work of genius as after Adebayor headed down, he span and hit a ball through a packed penalty area, and with Petr Cech unsighted, Arsenal had stolen a win. There was an outcry after the game that van Persie's first was blatantly offside – and maybe it was – but the important thing was that he had played to the whistle. No whistle was ever blown and he made his Chelsea counterparts pay the price. Wenger beamed afterwards: 'It was a test of character and we came here with perhaps not the needed level of confidence – but we have shown that we have character.'

Van Persie put in another excellent shift in a 1-0 home win against West Brom and was unlucky to see a couple of excellent shots blocked. He made up for that with a tremendous solo goal in a Man of the Match performance at home to Liverpool before an Adebayor red card and injury to Fàbregas saw them limp to a 1-1 draw. It was a shame that such a fantastic goal could not win the match as he chested down a pass and turned to create space before rifling home.

Van Persie said Adebayor had not deserved a red card and was thrilled to have scored a spectacular 10th goal of the season. He said: 'We all fought right until the end and if you look at the goal it was a very nice one – just one touch on my chest before I used my 'chocolate leg' as we say back home. It ended up in the corner of the net so yes, it was a good goal.'

He was in a good run of form and was desperately unfortunate to see a side-footed effort crash off the post in the gripping 2-2 Boxing Day draw at Villa Park. It was a fantastic start to 2009 for van Persie as he was picked to captain the side for the very first time. It was a great honour that the player who had let his side down so badly with that red card at Southampton all those years ago was now considered important enough in the team that he could skipper the side.

As van Persie later told Arsenal TV, he was a man who only wanted to be the best. He said: 'I just do things that I can do the best in. If I am unable to do drawing, I don't draw. This is how I am and if I try and try at something and it does not work, I say, "See you later".' He had tried for many years to be the best at Arsenal and had finally earned the captain's armband as a reward. There was no 'see you later' in sight.

Van Persie always was the man for big occasions and he failed to disappoint as he capped wearing the hallowed armband with two goals. Arsenal ran out 3-1 winners over Championship side Plymouth Argyle at the Emirates in a feisty cup tie. An unstoppable van Persie burst into the penalty area unmarked to meet the ball with a stooping header and open the scoring just after the break. Captain fantastic then showcased the unselfish attitude that had won him the captaincy when set up Nicklas Bendtner for the second goal. He rounded off a dominant display by pinging a powerful shot into the net after dancing a merry jig around the Pilgrims' goalkeeper.

It had been a complete surprise for van Persie to be handed the armband – Wenger took the decision because his regular captains were not involved in the game. Regular skipper Cesc Fàbregas was injured and his deputy, goalkeeper Manuel Almunia, was on the bench. After the game van Persie said: 'I was quite surprised when the manager said it, but I love it because I always just try to help and be positive for the team. It is just a great honour to be captain even if it is for just one game.'

Arsène Wenger said van Persie was the perfect choice for captain because of the role he played in the squad. Shouting might not have been his forte but van Persie always had an opinion on how things could be done better. Wenger told the *Examiner*: 'Robin is one of the leaders in the dressing room. He is not so much of a shouter but he speaks his mind. The Dutch way is to speak your mind and that is good but I must say he has fantastic humility as well. He listens to your opinion and is enjoyable to manage.'

Van Persie was the main man for the Gunners again as his spectacular last-minute volley rescued a point for the side in a 1-1 draw at Everton. Incredibly he had either scored or set up every goal Arsenal scored in January and was crowned 'Player of the Month' for the third month running. Wenger told the club website that van Persie's game had been improved greatly at the start of his Arsenal career by playing alongside his role model Dennis Bergkamp. The age of the two had been fortunate as it allowed Bergkamp to act like a father figure to a young man who clearly respected him and was keen to learn.

He said: 'At the start we gave him Dennis Bergkamp as a role model and he is growing into that role very well. Just look at the numbers. He is more of a goalscorer than Dennis and I think he has developed his vision and passing well. Robin respected Dennis and listened to his advice. He arrived when Dennis was already 33, 34, so he accepted to play that kind of master advice role. It was not anymore about van Persie taking his place. He wanted to help him.'

He agreed that van Persie had become marginalised towards the end of his spell at Feyenoord but that Arsenal were not deterred by his relegation to the bench and eventually the reserves by Bert van Marwijk. It was clear the team at Arsenal had faith in his ability to get past this setback and mature into an even better player. It was his passion for football that had brought him to this point, according to Wenger.

He continued: 'I believe that Robin is passionate about

the game. He was a little bit sidelined in Holland when we bought him and during the first year we observed him when he was more on the bench. In fact we watched him more in the Reserves than in the first team. When he arrived here it was a big move for him physically and mentally but I believe he has survived because of his talent and his intelligence but mainly because of his passion for the game. He wanted absolutely to make it. He has developed less on his individual talent than as a team player. '

Van Persie, however, was a less enthusiastic individual than he had been in his younger days. He was happy to have been doing so well for his club and had always said playing football was the most important thing in his life. Not anymore, however, as family man van Persie revealed that he had closed ranks somewhat in recent years. He said: 'I have learned that the world is rough. You must focus only on things that are important to you. That is crucial. And with all due respect, there are not a lot of things that are important. My family is. Besides that there are many who jump the bandwagon. Once you realize that not everything is nice and friendly, you'll become a lot calmer.

'Whenever I can make somebody happy I will. I used to try and keep everybody happy. But I cannot change the world. That has been a turning point. I have started to focus on my job and my family. That's it.'

Back to the action and van Persie netted a late effort as Arsenal progressed to the next round of the FA Cup with a 4-0 win over Championship side Cardiff City. They had hit a brick wall in the league, however, and drew three consecutive games 0-0 and slipped to a poor fifth position.

It looked as though it would be another fruitless

campaign in the Premier League but van Persie struck against AS Roma to continue their good run in the Champions League. He was hacked down after ghosting into the box and van Persie picked himself up to slam home the resulting spot kick to give Arsenal a 1-0 win.

Another brilliant performance from van Persie guided Arsenal through to an FA Cup semi-final at Wembley after a late rally helped them see off troublesome Hull City. Van Persie smacked into the net after finding space brilliantly, and took his tally to 16 for the season.

After a brilliant 3-0 second leg win over Villarreal, Arsenal also found themselves in the semi-finals of the Champions League. Van Persie had a terrific free-kick pushed away from danger before setting up Adebayor for the second goal of the night, and he finished the Spaniards off by scoring a late penalty. The contest was extremely easy on the eye with both sides out to play beautiful football. Wenger was pleased to see his team come out on top in a thoroughly entertaining game. He said: 'We sent out a very offensive team and we played in a convincing way. I was very impressed with the quality and speed of our game.'

The win set up an all-English semi-final showdown with Manchester United, which was a showdown Arsenal were relishing, according to Wenger.

That would prove to be van Persie's last chance of silverware this season as they were well out of the picture at the top of the Premier League and that man Didier Drogba was once again there to beat them in the FA Cup semi-final. Walcott had put his side ahead but Chelsea eventually ran out 2-1 winners, with van Persie having gone extremely close on several occasions.

He was extremely annoyed after the game and declared that the Gunners needed to get their stuff together before the Champions League final. He said: 'Every experience makes you stronger, a good one and definitely a bad one. We have to look game by game, because if you look at the schedule from now until the end of the season, it makes you a bit dizzy because we have big games every three or four days.'

Van Persie missed the away leg of the Champions League semi-final through injury but bounced back to claim a starting place in the return game at the Emirates with United leading 1-0. Despite van Persie's late goal, Arsenal were not good enough for United and were comfortably beaten 3-1 on their own patch. They had been second best all night and by the time van Persie had hammered a penalty into the net the damage had already been done by United and it was another season with nothing to show for all that brilliant football Arsenal had played.

Wenger said winning the Champions League had become his obsession but he would have to regroup his squad and try again next season. They never looked like beating United and would have to buck up their ideas if they ever wanted to lift the great trophy. For van Persie another fruitless season meant that at the age of 24, the incredibly gifted player had not added any trophies to his relatively bare footballing CV that only included winning the FA Cup and UEFA Cup.

Arsène Wenger would have been relieved to see van Persie sign a new contract in the summer that kept him at the club until 2014. There had been fears that he would leave the club and spark a mass exodus of stars from the Emirates with players growing disillusioned after a string of fruitless seasons in North London. Teenage stars Jack Wilshere, Aaron Ramsey and Kieran Gibbs all signed new deals after Wenger had convinced them the club would be able to win trophies with their help.

As he approached his mid-twenties, van Persie was feeling comfortable at Arsenal and insisted the club was more than capable of winning silverware in the upcoming season. The new deal was reported to be worth something in the region of £80,000 a week. He said: 'I have been at the club for five years now and there really is a great feeling here at Arsenal. We have a top-class manager, a squad full of superb young players, a world-class stadium and brilliant supporters. Arsenal have a very bright future and I want to be part of it.'

As they started the 2009/10 season with a thumping 6-1 win at Everton, Arsenal fans began to wonder if Wenger had been talking sense all along and the young stars might finally do something with all their talent. Van Persie set up two of the side's goals and twice went close with free-kicks as the Gunners turned on the style in Merseyside.

He had been unable to find the back of the net so far in the season but van Persie played an important role as Arsenal scored 15 goals in their first four matches of the season. After all that good work the Gunners again fell down when faced with the challenge of beating Manchester United.

When they were again losers just days later in a visit to Manchester City, the Gunners were already falling off the pace at the top of the Premier League. They were beaten 4-2 at Eastlands, but it had been looking like a good afternoon for van Persie as he had finally broken his duck for the season with a classic eye-catching strike. He span sneakily away from Joleon Lescott and smashed the ball into the bottom corner before Shay Given could react. It was a tense afternoon as Emmanuel Adebayor had left Arsenal for City in a summer storm. The pressure had been simmering all game but it boiled over in spectacular style when van Persie flew into a late, rash sliding tackle on his former team mate. Adebayor had done well to whip the ball away from van Persie's lunge, but as the Dutchman slid to the ground, the City man swung out his right boot and kicked him in the face. He had tried to make the movement appear to be part of his stride but it was fooling nobody. On that night's BBC *Match of the Day*, pundit Alan Shearer said it was an ugly incident and both men had deserved a red card. In the end it was only the City man who saw red.

Adebayor later claimed he had apologised to van Persie on the pitch but the Dutchman said that not only had he not received an apology, he would never get one in the future either. When asked if he saw a 'sorry' lurking on the horizon, van Persie said: 'Not any more. What can I say? I think he showed how he is in the last couple of weeks.'

Van Persie moved on from his spat with Adebayor when he netted in the next match at Fulham, this time starring as he scored the only goal of the game. Van Persie ran onto a lofted pass from Cesc Fàbregas before controlling with his left foot then burying it beyond Mark Schwarzer with his right. It was another top-drawer goal from van Persie as his technical ability secured all three points. Arsenal rookie goalkeeper Vito Mannone pulled off a string of saves to safeguard the win and steal the headlines from van Persie somewhat.

Van Persie was looking unstoppable as he hit another in a 2-0 Champions League win over Olympiacos. Eduardo held up play well, before van Persie made a late burst into the box to put the ball away. In his next match, at home to Blackburn Rovers, the striker scored for the ninth time in eight games as Arsenal powered to a 6-2 victory. In an Emirates goalfest, Fàbregas pulled the ball back smartly and van Persie struck a shot so firmly that Robinson had no chance of stopping it. Had he been stood right behind the effort, he would have been propelled into the net in the same way that the ball had been.

Life was bliss for van Persie at present and he celebrated the birth of his second child Dina Layla by opening the scoring in a 3-1 victory as Birmingham City were outplayed at the Emirates. After Alex Song headed the ball down to his feet, van Persie did very well to get the ball out of his feet and slip a shot into the net.

After the game he said to the *Irish Examiner* that despite a lack of sleep, his life was enhanced greatly by the arrival of his daughter and that having children gave him and Bouchra something to base their lives around. 'My family life is fantastic,' he said. 'The main things are my two kids and my wife and it makes you stable. It gives you a basis to perform because it is not good to go out all the time.'

After setting up Fàbregas brilliantly in the Champions League group game at AZ Alkmaar, van Persie hit another spectacular volley in the 2-2 draw at West Ham to make it six goals for the season. He also nudged a diving header just wide of the mark in another commanding Upton Park performance.

He had been on top form at the start of the season and a brace in the 3-0 humbling of Spurs made van Persie an even more popular man at the Emirates Stadium. He opened the scoring just before the break after beating Ledley King to a Bacary Sagna cross before Fàbregas added a second just seconds later. It was a comic third goal as the ball pin-balled around the area with Ledley King and goalkeeper Heurelho Gomes unable to get a grip on it. The ball bounced off van Persie and ended up in the net.

Spurs well and truly raised their white flag after van Persie put Arsenal in the lead. Man of the Match van Persie told Sky Sports his goal had stunned Tottenham and they never looked like coming back from it: 'It was quite tight and tough in the first half hour because we both went for it. From the moment we scored our first goal, they died basically – straight after Cesc Fàbregas scored an amazing goal.'

He was really enjoying playing in that central role, as the goalscoring charts proved. Van Persie told the Arsenal match day programme: 'I've had to get used to the new role because I previously played as a second striker, so I needed to find my way in. Earlier in the season, I lost too much energy working defensively and needed to find the right balance. It's really important for the team that I have enough energy to score goals and make assists, as well as helping out in other ways.'

That humiliation of Spurs was to prove his last meaningful action of the season for Arsenal after he suffered ankle ligament damage whilst on international duty. The Dutch were playing Italy in a friendly when a Giorgio Chiellini challenge left van Persie falling badly on his right ankle and resulted in him being stretchered off the field. Doctors had initially suggested he would only miss six weeks of action and van Persie was bullish about a comeback.

He would do anything to get fit and so when he was told about a new alternative therapy that was supposed to help injuries heal quicker, van Persie nipped off to Belgrade so that the famous Mariana Kovacevic could massage horses' placental fluid onto the injured ankle. These types of alternative therapy were roundly rubbished back in England but van Persie was not fussed about what people might say. Manchester City players Pablo Zabaleta, Nigel de Jong and Vincent Kompany had all been impressed by the results after visiting Kovacevic, so van Persie thought he would give it a go.

When he spoke to the BBC ahead of heading to Serbia for the treatment, van Persie sounded far from convinced that it would work. It showed how desperate he was to be a part of the team again that he would travel all this way for what could have been a meaningless exercise. He said: 'She is vague about her methods but I know she massages you using fluid from a placenta. I have been in contact with Arsenal physiotherapists and they have let me do it. I am going to try because it cannot hurt and, if it helps, it helps.'

Horse placenta or no horse placenta, the recovery did not go well and before he knew it van Persie had seen another important season pass him by. Wenger firmly believed things would have been different with van Persie spearheading the attack for the whole campaign.

As the 2009/10 season drew to a close in the spring, Arsenal supporters were left wondering what might have been if van Persie had been fit for the whole season. After trailblazer van Persie led the way in an exhilarating start that saw beautiful football win plaudits and points alike,

Arsenal dropped off badly and ended the season in third place, 10 points behind second-placed Manchester United and 11 behind champions Chelsea. Speaking to Arsenal TV during the squad's traditional end of season 'lap of appreciation', van Persie said the side had been great in patches but had just not been consistent enough to challenge for honours.

He said: 'We had great periods. In some we were not enough but I think we showed again that we can play some great football. We played third in a fantastic league, which is not bad, you know.' Van Persie heard his name sung loudly and proudly by the supporters on his lap round the ground and it would have provided some comfort.

Wenger was clearly a firm believer in the abilities of the Dutchman and compared him to some of the biggest players in the game today. He told the *Independent*: 'He had started to compete as one of the best players in the world and suddenly he was out. Would we have been talking about him alongside Lionel Messi, Cristiano Ronaldo and Wayne Rooney if he had not been injured? You would have talked about Van Persie in that company; of that I am sure. He can give a final ball, score goals and is good on set pieces. He is a leader because he has a football brain and is a football thinker. He has matured a lot in the last three or four years as well.'

The comment about him maturing showed that Wenger had known van Persie was far from the complete package when he initially signed and it was his way of saying 'I was right', even if his injuries had prevented van Persie from making the impact he may have had otherwise. When they had signed him from Feyenoord van Persie was a bright prospect with serious problems which Wenger clearly believed Arsenal would be able to exorcise.

He was part of a team that were sweeping all aside, scoring 36 goals in 11 league games. Without van Persie the team had gone on to lose three of their next four matches.

Despite the disappointment of losing him for most of the season, Wenger was optimistic van Persie would have a good World Cup and be back better than ever for the start of the next season in August. He said: 'When I pick a player it means he's fit and sharp. Robin lacks match practice, but physically he's fit. There's always a gamble but he's stronger and looking good for the future of his career. What is most satisfying for me is that, in training, he looks as if he hasn't been out. Overall, I don't believe we have been unlucky this year. I believe the team has shown unbelievable mental strength and has shown it has made a big step forward.'

Arsenal had all but blown any hope of regaining the Premier League title as they trailed 2-0 at White Hart Lane when van Persie came on with just over 20 minutes left. A stunning volley from Danny Rose on his Premier League debut and a strike from rising star Gareth Bale had already done the damage by the time van Persie came on the pitch but his introduction did spark life into the Gunners. When Abou Diaby flicked the ball into the area, van Persie chested the ball down and drew a spectacular save from goalkeeper Heurelho Gomes with a powerful volley. The Brazilian goalkeeper was not to be beaten and he tipped away a van Persie free-kick before pushing a Sol Campbell header onto the bar as it turned out not to be Arsenal's night, or Arsenal's season, once again.

CHAPTER 7
SO CLOSE

Once you have succeeded it is all too easy to forget the people who helped get you there. At the 2010 World Cup van Persie had something in common with Brazil's Michel Bastos, Australia's Brett Holman, the Ivory Coast's Salomon Kalou, South Koran Kim Nam-Il and Dane Patrick Mtiliga. They had all played for Excelsior. That tiny club had played a big part in shaping six of the world's best and without his time there, who knows where van Persie would have been in 2010?

Surely the highlight of any player's career would be representing their country at a World Cup, and with that little bit more experience than at his last tournament, van Persie had a much more realistic chance of taking the trophy home. South Africa 2010 was an unusual tournament in which many big names fell at the first hurdle, nearly everybody moaned about having to use bouncy footballs, and incessant blowing of horn-like vuvuzelas saw paracetamol sales rocket.

It didn't take much to get van Persie into the mood. He told the Scottish *Daily Record* he had become obsessed with the World Cup in the lead-up to the tournament and even had a poster of Diego Maradona holding the trophy on a wall at home. He said: 'I have a really big picture of Maradona in my games room. If we win I want that picture with me holding the World Cup and hopefully scoring the winner. The amount of hard work I have put in [during his rehabilitation] was incredible. I just know if my body is in good shape, I don't have to worry about a thing on the pitch.'

As we've a already seen the Dutch had a history of inter-team rifts ruining chances at tournaments and in the build-up to the South African tournament, van Persie was hardly doing his best to keep the peace. When asked questions about the 'big four' players – himself, Arjen Robben, Wesley Sneijder and Rafael Van der Vaart – he did not stop and say everyone was in it together, he accepted as fact that they were the best. He might not have understood what the interviewer meant, he might not have been paying attention, but he still went along with it. This kind of behaviour could well have put his place in the team under threat as coach van Marwijk would have been far from amused.

Not content with going along with the idea that four members of his team were better players than the rest, van Persie then made the somewhat naive statement that he would rather play alongside Rafael van der Vaart than Dirk Kuyt. From the outside it must have looked like he was doing his best to put his foot in it and the Dutch camp looked set for another tournament of egotistic clashes.

Had there been a more hard-line manager in charge – Sir Alex Ferguson or Roy Keane, for example – he would probably have been dumped out of the team. Although he did not say it, the idea was put to him as fact and this was the kind of behaviour to be expected from the 'problem child' van Persie of old, not the grown-up, well-measured van Persie of 2010.

Although this incident was glossed over, the threat of it becoming an issue highlights the dangers posed to players by speaking to the press. So much can be read into what players say, it is surprising that teams have not imposed tighter restrictions. For better or worse, the various forms of media have a huge impact on footballers and their actions on the pitch. The England national team, for example, appeared out of focus for the entire tournament and that might well have had something to do with John Terry being stripped of the captain's armband after the *News of the World* uncovered his affair with team mate Wayne Bridge's then-girlfriend.

Nothing more was said – maybe van Marwijk wanted to react but did not want to lose one of his star men just before a major tournament was due to get underway. Maybe he would have a word in van Persie's ear or kick up a fuss about it publicly once the World Cup was over.

Former Netherlands international Ronald Koeman summed up the importance of a fully-fit van Persie to club and country when he brought AZ Alkmaar to the Emirates Stadium for a Champions League group match before the striker suffered his injury. He said: 'At the moment he is our best Dutch player, he shows that every week for Arsenal.'

Former Chelsea player manager Ruud Gullit, who won the

European Championships with the Dutch in 1988, believed the fact that van Persie's season had been hampered by injury could work to his country's advantage in the tournament.

Feeling optimistic before the tournament started, Gullit told the *Daily Star*: 'Van Persie will be a big star for us because I see the same pattern I did with Marco van Basten. He was injured in 1988 and then he came back into shape. We ended up doing very well, and he was the reason. He was that good at that moment. It could be an advantage for the Netherlands that van Persie was injured and he now comes back. He's fresh, eager, hungry. He doesn't want his rest, he wants to play, to score goals.

'Van Persie's injury was a tragedy for him, and for Arsenal it was bad also. But for Holland it was maybe a good thing. I spoke with him recently, and saw him in Holland when he was trying to come back from his injury. He looks very good. It's difficult to score a lot of goals at the World Cup and I think you will have to score six or seven to be the top scorer. But he could do it.'

Gullit was making sense – he had seen the same thing happen with van Basten and it was a valid point – a lot of other players were coming from intense seasons straight into the finals and this gave van Persie a clear advantage.

In stark contrast to the class of 2006, this Netherlands squad was a mature one – the squad had an average age of 27.7. This set of players had played in big competitions before and knew what it was all about. They were unlikely to wilt under pressure and this mental steel would no doubt help their cause.

As van Persie lined up in Soccer City for his side's opening group match on 14 June, lifting the FIFA World Cup trophy must have seemed a long way off. It may have been far away in terms of matches they would need to win and in that it was four weeks until the final, but geographically at least, he was already there. The Netherlands' game against Denmark took place in Soccer City stadium in Johannesburg, which was to host the final.

The game took a while to get going in what was a slow start for most teams in South Africa. There were disgruntled mutterings about the noise from vuvuzelas – a horn that sounded like a swarm of angry bees when blown by fans – upsetting the rhythm of the game. Van Persie, under the watchful eye of Johan Cruyff, who had been picked out by the television cameras, made only two contributions of note in the opening period. First he controlled skilfully with his chest to set up Wesley Sneijder whose shot was blocked, before he showed good feet to move inside and have a shot himself – but that was also blocked.

The Danish defence was finally breached just after the second half had got underway and it was a goal of van Persie's making. As he chased a through ball, which was heading away from goal, Denmark goalkeeper Thomas Sørensen rushed out to intercept the ball. Van Persie did brilliantly to take the ball away from the advancing green figure and ran towards the left-hand touchline as he stopped the ball from going out of play. He turned back from the goal line, shaped up to cross with his right foot, then turned and delivered a cross with his left foot. Despite no Dutch player being near him, Christian Poulsen headed the ball into the back of fellow defender Daniel Agger and it bounced into the net.

It might not have been scored by a Dutch player but they all count and van Persie had already made a goal for his country in the 2010 World Cup. It seemed all the players were taking a while to find their stride and the usually clinical van Persie was the same – his first touch hadn't been there when he was bearing down on Sørensen's goal and the ball bounced into the goalkeeper's hands.

Much like he had done for Arsenal that season, van Persie's main role in the opening game was as the man players could play passes into and receive passes from. The stats spoke for themselves – he had a 95 per cent success rate. Dirk Kuyt of Liverpool was also impressive and sealed a 2-0 win when he tapped-in from close range.

Van Marwijk was far from impressed with the way his side played, despite a 2-0 victory. He told a post-match press conference: 'We tried to play beautiful football but we kept losing the ball. From time to time you could see how good it could be.'

It's one thing to say things could get better, but it is another to actually make things better. After his calamitous error cost England a win in their opening round 1-1 draw with the USA, goalkeeper Robert Green was dropped to the bench by manager Fabio Capello. Van Marwijk did not have the 'luxury' of an obvious scapegoat (his team had also just won 2-0 and England had drawn), so he had no real option other than to have a quiet word in players' ears and think about making a few tweaks to his formation.

If the teams were reconsidering their open relationship with the media, the journalists were probably also thinking long and hard about the arrangement after Dirk Kuyt made this car-crash of a joke in the build-up to their second group match against Japan: 'Lots of players on our team eat sushi and we hope we will have them for dinner.' Perhaps Dutch humour is as acquired a taste as sushi itself.

Van Persie again led from the front in Durban and found himself being hauled down by Daisuke Matsui in the first 10 minutes. It was certainly a heated encounter as the Japanese refused to lie down for their more illustrious opponents. The Dutch became frustrated in the first half as 11 Japanese men sat behind the ball made it hard for them to build any kind of move. Japan defender Yuji Nakazawa felt the force of van Persie's frustration – the Dutchman somewhat foolishly putting his hands around his opposite number's throat and fortunate to avoid recriminations beyond conceding a free-kick.

Van Persie could have opened the scoring early in the second half but still couldn't find his World Cup scoring boots. Giovanni van Bronckhorst nutmegged his man before delivering an inviting cross from the left, but van Persie was a little too far forward and he was forced to back-peddle to reach it. He did well to make a connection and direct the ball towards goal but that backward movement took all the power out of his header and served more to comfortably cushion it towards the goalkeeper in the way a defender would.

Wesley Sneijder finally put the Dutch in front after van Persie had done brilliantly to control the ball in the box (despite the slight suspicion that he used his hand) with his back to goal. He laid it off to Sneijder who lashed a powerful shot that Eiji Kawashima could only get a hand to and the ball crashed into the net. Three Netherlands goals so far in the tournament and van Persie was behind two of them. The new ball being used for the tournament, the Adidas Jabulani, was heavily criticised throughout and this was the first time the Dutch were caught up in the debate – many neutrals thought the ball's trademark unpredictable flight was the undoing of Kawashima.

Everton defender Johnny Heitinga said in an interview with the *Daily Star* later in the tournament that the unpredictable flight of the ball had helped players like Sneijder. He said: 'Sneijder can score goals from far out, especially with this crazy Jabulani ball.' As many a wise man said during the tournament, the ball may have been unpredictable but it was the same for every team – they all had to deal with its behaviour. In some games, like the Netherlands against Japan, the victors would be the team who adapted to the ball better.

The Dutch main man wasn't afraid of doing things the ugly way when he needed to – booting a Yasuhito Endo corner clear. Despite the best efforts of Nigel De Jong, who nearly conceded a penalty in stoppage time with a slightly over-zealous tackle, the Dutch closed out the game and made it two wins out of two.

The Netherlands had hardly been playing their most attractive football and van Marwijk said to CBC Sports after the win over Japan: 'Why do we focus on good football instead of winning? Let me assure you that we really, really want to win and if we can do that in style, then great, but you have to be able to win ugly games.'

Flair players like van Persie and Sneijder appeared alongside tougher propositions Nigel De Jong and Johnny Heitinga to give the side a real balance between beautiful moves and crunching tackles to 'get the business done'.

Indeed, this seemed a far meaner Dutch side than in previous years and van Persie himself was showing he had more to his game than just fancy touches as he tackled tough and pushed hard.

Johnny Heitinga joined the call for a 'new' Netherlands, with the side clearly keen to leave their reputation for attractive, ultimately unsuccessful football behind them. He told the *Daily Star*: 'We now all have to seize the moment. In the past, people have said that the Dutch team play nice football and we are always admired for our movement. But then we never win anything. We know that all too well and want to change that.'

Van Persie was still to find the net in the tournament. He appeared to struggle with the Jabulani ball, which used an aerodynamic system to give it a much more random movement than the 'powerful and accurate' Nike Total 90 Ascente, which had been used in the Premier League the previous season. Free-kicks were a particular let-down in this World Cup and van Persie, usually deadly when wrapping his left foot around the ball from 25 or so yards, had not even come close to scoring one. Rafael van der Vaart, who was to earn a move to Tottenham Hotspur with an eye-catching performance in the tournament, was taking free-kicks and van Persie was not even getting a sniff.

The English-based players were at a slight disadvantage to players from other domestic leagues, which had introduced the ball during the 2009/10 season. Players from leagues such as the Bundesliga in Germany were able to steal a march on Premier League players by spending the season getting used to the flight and behaviour of the Jabulani.

As they lined up to face Cameroon in their final group game, the Netherlands were perhaps now the dark horses of the tournament. They had hardly shone brightly in the first two games but picked up wins in both without really making people sit up and take notice.

With van Persie scoring no goals in the first two games, he was under real pressure to find the back of the net. He was, after all, leading the line for the Dutch and although he had been the creative brains behind the majority of their best moves and goals, people would soon start asking questions if he did not contribute goals himself.

In Cape Town van Persie finally opened his 2010 World Cup account. His connection with Sneijder looked sharper than in previous games and good combination play saw both go close in the opening stages. Second choice goalkeeper Souleymanou Hamidou was quick off his line to smother as van Persie latched onto a through ball with just eight minutes gone. Van Persie was getting closer and he was again put through by Sneijder before shooting but the shot was straight at the advancing blue figure of Hamidou.

Perhaps Jonathan Liew of the *Telegraph* was getting a bit carried away when he suggested van Persie and Sneijder had been 'raised by the same family of outstandingly gifted deer' but his strangely-worded proposal made a valid point. The two were really starting to click and maybe this would be the kind of service Arsenal fans could come to expect if he ever stayed clear of injury for long enough to build an understanding with his team mates.

Ten minutes before half-time van Persie finally made his mark when he combined beautifully with van der Vaart to create an opening. After finding himself crowded out on the right-hand flank, van Persie danced a jig in front of Cameroon left-back and Tottenham rival Benoit Assou-Ekotto before turning away from goal and playing infield to van der Vaart. As the Cameroon left-back stood and watched, van Persie made a darting move inside him and towards goal, where an inch-perfect dink saw him slip through the rearguard and baring down on Hamidou's goal. Kuyt jumped out of the way and van Persie's right foot fired the ball through the goalkeeper's legs – no sweat. The creative geniuses embraced in the corner of the pitch and the Netherlands were well on the way to topping their group.

That extra piece of sharpness and movement van Persie was able to find might well have had something to do with the fact he had missed large chunks of the season – just as the great orange prophet Ruud Gullit had predicted. Assou-Ekotto had racked up 34 appearances as Tottenham fought their way to Champions League qualification whilst van Persie had missed a lot of the season after that Giorgio Chiellini challenge.

There was talk that van Persie was still not 100 per cent fit and when he hit yet another shot straight at Hamidou, perhaps it was showing. His team mates clearly didn't have full confidence in their front-man as van der Vaart shared free-kick taking responsibilities with Sneijder. The effectiveness of van Persie's trademark curling efforts was nullified by the free-spirited Jabulani ball so the Dutch adopted a new tactic that other teams had chosen to employ. It was a far cry from getting an effort over a wall and dipping it back down towards the goal, but many teams chose to play the percentages and play a ball that would go over the wall and then bounce in front of the goalkeeper. The Jabulani bounce was so unpredictable that it would often be hard to catch and a number of players would swamp the six-yard box in an attempt to bundle the ball home.

After netting his first goal of the finals, van Persie was then forced to make way for Arjen Robben, another big-name forward who was on the way back from injury problems of his own. Robben was injured in a World Cup build-up friendly and his creativity had been sorely missed by the Dutch. But without van Persie the team immediately conceded their first goal of the tournament. Van der Vaart lifted an arm to protect his face from a Geremi free-kick and 29-year-old Samuel Eto'o gratefully smashed home the resulting penalty kick.

If that was something van Persie didn't really want to see, what happened next wouldn't have exactly filled his heart with joy either. Robben – the man who replaced him – created a chance from nothing and rifled a shot against the post. Klaas-Jan Huntelaar was ready to pounce and opportunistically swept the ball into an unguarded net.

The Netherlands had won three games out of three and van Persie had played a big part in their progress from Group E. Yet the team had only showed their flamboyant side on isolated occasions and at times played in a brutal fashion. The hordes of orange fans were pleased to see their team progress but had hardly been blown away by what they had seen. Van Marwijk said the defensive lapse which led to Cameroon's equaliser was a period of negligence that they could not afford to let happen again.

Perhaps the team had chosen to save their best performances for later in the competition. Maybe they had learned from the mistakes of Euro 2008 when they started so brightly but became jaded and their challenge faded away. Various players told the press they were not too worried about the team's unattractive displays but, always a man to speak his mind, van Persie broke from the ranks to promise supporters the side had a lot more to offer. He told the *Times* that his side's performances were set to improve as they reached the knockout stages in South Africa.

He said: 'I hope we have a lot more to come in the tournament. After the first three games we know we can play to a higher standard. But you can see that here and there we play some fantastic football and we have the right intentions. Attractive and attacking football is how we like to play.'

With the successful return of Robben to the team, a storm was brewing. Who was going to be left out of the starting line-up? Van Persie's place was under threat and something had to give. His pre-tournament remarks about who he would rather play alongside could well come back to haunt van Persie, and who would blame a strong-minded coach for making a loud-mouth player pay for his words?

Former Netherlands player Bolo Zenden told the *Times*: 'The players are mature enough to handle things like van Persie's misquoted comments on Kuyt. Seven players were part of the team in Euro 2004. Mark van Bommel is a very important influence in the team: he's not the captain, but you don't need an armband to be a leader.

'When Arjen Robben gets back to full fitness, then Bert Van Marwijk might have to cut someone out, and then we'll see what the reaction is. As long as the results are there, everyone knows their place. But when things aren't going your way, that's when you see what kind of characters you have. But the vibe is good now.'

The vibe was indeed good but there was trouble on the horizon for the Dutch, who were still only 7/1 to win the tournament. If they were able to beat Slovakia in their second-round game, the possibility of a meeting with Brazil in the quarter-finals loomed ominously in the distance.

They had to beat Slovakia first and van Persie knew that was not going to be an easy task in itself. It was hard to ignore their European brothers after they had beaten Italy 3-2 in the last round to put the four-time World Cup winners out of the competition. Van Persie told a press conference: 'Slovakia will be very tough. They showed really good spirit and hung in there against Italy and it was a great result for their country. So far, it's looking good, but we can still improve on bits and pieces.'

When the team sheet was published, van Persie would have breathed a sigh of relief that it was Rafael van der Vaart who was dropped in favour of Arjen Robben and he was set to continue upfront. So long as he was still in the team, van Persie would not be too jealous of his team mate.

In the fifth minute Dirk Kuyt (playing ahead of van der Vaart, which would not have pleased van Persie) delivered an inviting cross which van Persie really should have buried. Instead he slightly misjudged the flight of the ball and miscued his header. It should have been 1-0 with 10 minutes gone when van Persie skipped his way through the defence before unselfishly laying off to Sneijder who was not quite in tune and caught the ball at the wrong moment.

Robben opened the scoring with a skilful solo effort that

he blasted into the corner of the net. This was the most complete Dutch performance of the tournament so far. As van Persie had promised, things had got prettier – at one stage Nigel de Jong back-heeled a clearance to break up a Slovakian move.

Van Persie was doing everything right apart from finding the net. When put through by Mark Van Bommel, he was only able to swing a leg at the ball and send it horribly wide of the target. There were plenty of opportunities for him to score but these simply weren't being taken and van Persie was on his way to an unfavourable record of one goal in four matches. Those poor finishes bred frustration and left-back Radoslav Zabavnik was in the wrong place at the wrong time to feel the force of van Persie's anger. The pair collided in a crunching second-half challenge and the Slovakian came off worse with a heavy knock to the shin.

The Dutch made the game safe when goalkeeper Jan Mucha needlessly charged out to claim a ball he was never going to claim and Sneijder took full advantage with help from Kuyt. It was too little, too late when Robert Vittek scored a consolation penalty for Slovakia but it certainly shone light on some cracks in the Dutch defence. Their 'classic' performance was yet to come and van Persie's stock was gradually falling as he was not contributing what was expected of a man with 18 international goals to his name before the start of the tournament.

In yet another honest post-match interview, van Persie told reporters of his frustrations at failing to hit the back of the net. He said: 'I am not scoring and that eats away at me. I wanted to finish the Slovakia game as I thought they would take risks in the last 10 minutes and I could exploit that. I could see spaces opening up and wanted to use them so I was shocked when I had to go off. I'm doing my absolute best and desperately want to score and give assists but it hasn't worked out for me.'

It was clear that, despite his team reaching the quarter-final stage, all was not well in van Persie's mind. In the fallout from the game there were accusations that van Persie was angry at his 80th-minute substitution and it was reported he had told Bert van Marwijk that Wesley Sneijder should have been replaced instead. The coach said van Persie had not said this and publically backed the under-fire striker.

Sneijder, who stayed on the pitch to score the match-clinching second goal, said: 'Robin assured me that he had not said those words and I have no reason to doubt him. I don't have a problem with him and I never have done. He was disappointed to come off, that one can understand and it really isn't a serious matter. We will be united as never before against Brazil.'

That inter-squad bickering was clearly never going to leave the Dutch camp no matter what they said. It is unknown whether van Persie made that complaint, because the country would always want to present a united front. Van Marwijk would not want to risk players walking out on their team (as happened in their infamous 1994 World Cup dispute). Elsewhere, the French team famously walked out of training after former Arsenal man Nicolas Anelka was sent home from the tournament for an outburst at his manager Raymond Domenech.

The Dutch had a score to settle when they came up against the most celebrated team in international football – Brazil – at Nelson Mandela Bay Stadium. In van Persie's youth the country had been dumped out of successive World Cup tournaments by the Seleção. In the 1994 World Cup quarter-final, the Dutch had fought back from 2-0 down thanks to goals from Dennis Bergkamp and Aron Winter. They were beaten by a thunderbolt Branco free-kick at the death. It was even tighter in the 1998 semi-final in France when the two could not be separated by extra time as they drew 1-1 and the tie went to penalties. Phillip Cocu and Ronald de Boer both had strikes saved by Taffarel in the Brazil goal and the Oranje were beaten.

The Dutch now had to face this country, one of the tournament favourites and another nation famed for playing an attractive brand of football. Any lingering hopes that the Dutch would reprise their 'Total Football' style were snuffed out when van Marwijk said that the sport had moved on since then.

He told the BBC: 'It was a long time ago, Total Football – if you play like that now it's very hard to win the Cup.' The Netherlands' Total Football was back in 1974. We could play football very well for 20 or 30 years. It was Total Football, and I also remember Brazil's samba football. But sport changes and football changes also. It has to do with the fact everybody is getting fitter, better organised.'

So maybe modern football was too organised for that famous fluid, creative style of play to be a success. Expectations were not dampened by this statement and van Persie had a chance to prove that Total Football lived on after all.

The game started on a controversial note when van Persie felt he should have been awarded a penalty. Dirk Kuyt played an excellent lofted through-ball and central defender

Juan appeared to shove van Persie to the ground before winning possession. Japanese referee Yuichi Nishimura was far from convinced a foul had been committed and allowed play to continue. The Dutch continued their trademark early push as Robben tried to feed van Persie but the ball was shepherded out of play.

That bright start counted for nothing as once again van Persie failed to convert chances into goals and Manchester City's maverick striker Robinho showed him how it was done to put the Brazilians a goal up. Felipe Melo played a cutting pass and Robinho's crisp finish left the Dutch facing an uphill struggle if they wanted to make the semi-finals.

They nearly levelled the score straight away as van Persie set up Kuyt, whose shot was blocked by Julio Cesar. When he was finally given the chance to line up a free-kick 30 yards out – after Sneijder and van der Vaart had assumed responsibility for most of the finals – van Persie demonstrated why he had not been allowed to take one thus far. His effort had spectators behind the goal more worried than Julio Cesar. He was probably counting down the matches until he was rid of that Jabulani ball and back to the more conventional Nike footballs of the Premier League.

The Netherlands were struggling to get players on the ball at all as Brazil dominated for most of the first half. Van Persie's card was clearly marked as his every move was predicted and the ball promptly taken away from him. The front man was forced to move deeper and deeper to pick up possession and before half-time the star in the Dutch 'Christmas tree' was camped in his own half defending.

Brazil were so much on top that they were scoring for

both sides – Julio Cesar ran to gather a Sneijder cross he had no hope of getting anywhere near and the ball bounced off the head of Felipe Melo into his own net. With 20 minutes left the Dutch had stolen the lead despite being second best for most of the match. A Robben corner was nodded on by Kuyt and Sneijder headed home from two yards out. It was all too much for the dominant Brazilians to handle and so, not content with scoring an own goal, Melo saw fit to stamp on Sneijder's foot and was dismissed. Van Persie did nothing of note other than blaze another free-kick high, wide and not very handsome.

The final whistle blew and there were wild scenes as the Dutch squad jumped around madly in a huddle of celebration. Once again they had not played outstandingly but yet again they were victorious. The first major challenge to Brazil had seen their players lose their rags and eventually lose the game. Van Marwijk must have been doing something right, even if it was not initially obvious.

Whenever the Netherlands and Brazil have met each other in the World Cup, the winner has always gone on to reach the final. That was an encouraging statistic for the Dutch as they headed into their semi-final showdown with Uruguay as one of the favourites to lift the trophy.

Van Persie had fallen on his arm during the win in Port Elizabeth and he was sent to hospital for a scan to make sure there were no underlying problems. Van Marwijk told the BBC he wasn't sure what was wrong but the Dutch medical staff did not think it was too serious. He was also keen to rebuff claims his side were clear favourites against the South Americans. Complacency had been the undoing of the Netherlands many times in the past and their coach was doing his best to make sure it wasn't the case this time around.

Before the game he said: 'We just want to concentrate on ourselves, we don't want to be misled or distracted by people thinking we are the favourites. In the group phase, we were always the favourite, never the underdog. Against Brazil, it was the other way around. I don't really have an opinion on that.'

Tellingly, he praised members of the Dutch squad but left out van Persie, whose ego never really needs feeding and anyway had not been performing exceptionally well.

Van Marwijk said: 'Wesley Sneijder is playing an excellent tournament and we have others who are also doing well, but he is proving to be very sharp, very fit and he trained at 100 per cent from day one. Kuyt is another who is extremely important to us and will always give a lift to the other players. His passion and enthusiasm is catching. I am very happy with him. It is becoming harder as we are in the last four, our opponents will be tough. If we win with beautiful football, great, but we would be happier with a victory.'

His boss might not have mentioned his efforts but Johnny Heitinga was extremely complimentary about van Persie when speaking to the *Daily Star* – calling him one of the best players in the world. He said: 'Our forwards definitely have a lot of skill. In my mind, the four of them are the most fearsome attacking unit in the world. Van Persie, too, is one of the best players in the world. All the skills he has with his left foot, all the twisting and turning, are very effective and tie defenders into knots. I think any defender playing against van Persie, Robben, Sneijder and van der

Vaart will have trouble in coping with their speed, power and attacking abilities.'

They had told the world they were not underestimating Uruguay but the Dutch must have known they were very close to a first World Cup final appearance for four decades. It was the team who reached the tournament with eight wins out of eight in their qualifying group against the team who were last to seal a trip to South Africa when they won a play-off match.

Van Marwijk said before the game that Uruguay were survivors who would fight until the bitter end and so it proved in a thrilling Cape Town encounter. People say England is the 'home of football' and our nation is obsessed with the game, but the Dutch go that little bit further in the obsession stakes. Out of a population of 15 million people, it was estimated that 11.5 million had tuned in to watch their side (hopefully) progress to the World Cup final.

In amongst all the build-up, the thing that would have meant the world to van Persie was to receive a text from Arsène Wenger wishing him well ahead of the showdown. It is a great boost for anybody heading into a life-changing period in their life to know people are wishing them well. Van Persie has always enjoyed a somewhat complicated relationship with his coaches but he had matured so much in his time in North London and Wenger appeared to love him in the way that a father would stick by their well-meaning but sometimes wayward son.

Everything was going nicely to plan when a Giovanni Van Bronckhorst screamer put the Oranje one-nil up. Once again they were quick out of the blocks and this time it paid off for former Arsenal man Van Bronckhorst, who had announced he was to retire from the game after the World Cup. His 30-yard screamer bounced in off the post to get the party started.

The Dutch might have been winning but they were hardly in charge. Van Marwijk had warned that the South Americans were battlers and so it turned out that van Persie was hassled and harried every time he tried to get a move started. It was little wonder that the Uruguayans had reached this stage as they prevented the Netherlands from building much momentum and were dangerous on the counter attack themselves. The game was level going into the break after Diego Forlan, who had endured a frustrating spell at Manchester United from 2002 until 2004 but bounced back successfully in La Liga, chanced his luck with a 30-yard pot shot. Maarten Stekelenburg completely misjudged the flight of the ball and his flailing glove could not stop the ball on its path to the goal.

Van der Vaart came on at half-time to beef up the midfield but van Persie was still nowhere to be seen. In a similar style to Dennis Bergkamp in the 1998 semi-final defeat to Brazil, the flair man was wandering around on his own up front, looking lost and detached from the action.

In the 70th minute van Persie remembered where he was and suddenly looked interested again. It was little coincidence that his team regained the lead shortly afterwards when he cleverly stepped over Sneijder's low drive which bobbled its way into the net. With 15 minutes left the Netherlands were surely home and dry as Arjen Robben used his balding head to direct a powerful header into the far corner of the goal. That head was comically slapped in the resulting celebration and van Persie was seemingly heading to a World Cup final appearance, despite not making a great personal contribution to the team's progress.

The Dutch were coasting but something usually goes wrong for them and hearts were in mouths in the 90th minute when Max Pereira put in Uruguay's second with a neat finish from outside the box. For a few nerve-wracking minutes that final place which looked nailed-on before was suddenly in the balance. Van Persie was obviously startled by this and, even if he had waited until late in the game to do so, did eventually make a telling contribution.

Tracking back as the Dutch came under increasing pressure in the closing stages, he made a brilliant block from Egidio Arévalo's shot and the final whistle blew shortly afterwards. Everybody knew that van Persie had been far from his best in South Africa but he was poised to lead the Dutch attack in the World Cup final.

Van Marwijk said the secret to his team's success was that they did not become complacent in the way gifted Dutch teams of the past had done. He said: 'We have so often proved we can win matches against good opponents – if you really believe in something it can come true. At some point the members of the team started believing it and then we had to create the mentality of not being complacent. The players have started to understand this. Then, as now, you get an atmosphere in the team and I told them ahead of the match: "Don't let them get away with it".'

The Netherlands won a World Cup in 2010 thanks to a thrilling 4-2 victory over Wales. Unfortunately for Robin that tournament was the 'Cash Converters World Cup of Darts' in December and not the tournament in South

Africa. The grand finale between the Netherlands and Spain was built up as the ultimate footballing showdown in the days beforehand but, as is so often the way in showcase matches, failed to live up to the expectation.

Any World Cup final is one of the biggest games in a country's history but for both the Dutch and Spanish this was extra-special as they had the chance to win the tournament for the very first time. The pair have reputations as extraordinarily good footballing countries yet neither had won the biggest prize in international football. There was massive pressure on the Dutch – the national side had lost the final in both 1974 and 1978 with a squad of incredibly talented players. Johan Cruyff and his Total Football fell at the final hurdle against West Germany and Argentina respectively.

The fact that such a beautiful brand of football brought only runners-up medals must have played on the minds of the players and especially head coach Bert van Marwijk. Dutch teams had a reputation for playing beautiful attacking football and the class of 2010 were keeping that tradition going with 12 goals in the six games – an average of two goals a game – that got them to the final. The stage was set for van Persie to become a hero in his country. He had hardly had a classic tournament and only scored one goal but a match-winning performance would have secured legendary status in the eyes of the Dutch public.

Van Persie told a pre-tournament press conference the players from the great sides of those 1970s finals are greatly respected. He said: 'Playing in a World Cup Final means more than anything to me. You grew up with their names in your face. When those people say anything in the press or on a TV programme everybody listens because of what they achieved.'

There was a history of discontent within the Dutch national squad and whilst things did not boil over in the spectacular way they did in the past, there was talk of a rift between van Persie and Inter Milan's Wesley Sneijder – who had played for Feyenoord's arch nemeses Ajax whilst van Persie was still at De Kuip.

The KNVB was keen to quash any talk of unrest in the camp ahead of the game, so players gave somewhat forced sound bites telling the world they were the best of friends. Van Persie told reporters they should put cameras in the team hotel and watch team mates playing cards and cracking jokes with each other. He told the *Daily Star*: 'I believe we have the mental toughness now. Let's give the country the ultimate reason to celebrate.'

After a seemingly never-ending tedious build-up to the final itself, finally on Sunday 30 June it was time for action. The Dutch players marched out of the tunnel and van Persie had a look of hunger and concentration on his face as he marched past a television camera holding a young mascot's hand. He was set to start the 2010 World Cup final up front as the Dutch number nine with Sneijder directly behind him and the tasty proposition of crosses from Liverpool's Dirk Kuyt on the left-hand side and former Chelsea man Arjen Robben on the right. The poster of Diego Maradona holding the World Cup trophy aloft was sitting at home waiting for its owner to do the same thing.

As is so often the way when games are over-hyped, the match completely failed to live up to its somewhat optimistic billing as the most beautiful match in the history of football. National coach van Marwijk had obviously been influenced by the beautiful failures of those famous 1970s Dutch teams and decided that in an attempt to win, his team was to do things a different way – kick lumps out of their Spanish counterparts.

Van Persie led by example as he put the boot in several times during the opening exchanges and was booked as early as the 15th minute. Following wave after wave of Spanish attacks, goalkeeper Maarten Stekelenburg decided to punt the ball downfield to relieve some of the pressure. After failing to reach the kick, van Persie chased the ball down like a dog after a mechanical rabbit. Carles Puyol brought the ball down and spread to his left-back Joan Capdevila, who attempted to turn away and play around van Persie. The Dutch number nine had other ideas and slid in, deciding that he was either going to win the ball or take the man. It didn't appear too strong a challenge but, as is the way in the modern game, the Spaniard let out a cry so loud it could be picked up above the drone of the vuvuzelas by the pitch-side microphones and English referee Howard Webb marched over to flash the first yellow card of the game.

After the tournament, Webb said he had warned van Persie from the first minute of the game to be sensible and had no choice but to flash his card. He told the *Independent*: 'The game started OK. I warned Mark van Bommel and Robin van Persie in the first few minutes. I just said to them: "Remember where we are and what we are doing. Let's be sensible guys." It was all about getting the trust of the players – not overreacting but equally making sure I dealt with it. After two warnings we had two yellow cards in the first 16 minutes. I had no choice, having warned van Persie.'

Webb admitted it must have been hard for the players to control themselves as victory would make them history makers in their native countries. He said: 'Both sides were this close to being icons forever. Think about how we treat our 1966 team. Neither team had a star on their shirt and they wanted one. You could see in the first minute with the tackle van Persie put in on Sergio Busquets.'

Far from being the only booking of the game, van Persie's lunge set the standard in a game which clocked up an astonishing 13 yellow cards – plus a second yellow to Johnny Heitinga, who was dismissed. It was supposed to be one of the most attractive World Cup finals ever but the game would have appealed more to martial arts fans. Indeed Manchester City's Nigel de Jong was lucky to stay on the field after trying out his best Jackie Chan impression on Spain's Xabi Alonso.

Capdevila got his revenge in the second half when, with the game still goalless, Mark van Bommel spotted van Persie in a bit of space and played him through down the right. From a standing start, van Persie spun niftily away and charged towards goal but just as he started to break into a gallop, the left-back cynically clipped van Persie's heels to send him tumbling to the deck. One-all.

It was a game of few chances but van Persie gave Arjen Robben the perfect opportunity to win it at the death. With time running out the Dutch resorted to lumping the ball downfield and, although it is not the style of play an Arsenal star is used to, van Persie adapted well. He ran towards a hopeful kick from a deep Nigel de Jong and, unchallenged, flicked the ball into the path of Robben who was bearing down on goal. Carles Puyol was too slow for Robben and after trying but failing to grab onto his orange shirt, Puyol span around and hit the floor whilst advancing goalkeeper Iker Casillas smothered the ball.

The game ran into extra time and, with both sets of players tiring, Andrés Iniesta broke Dutch hearts. There would have been a tear rolling down the face of that picture of Maradona back in van Persie's house as the ball hit the back of the net followed by a euphoric Spanish celebration. As one commentator remarked, 'There will be no Dutch delight today'. One final push forward saw van Persie head unselfishly across the face of the six-yard box but nobody was there to meet it and Webb blew the final whistle.

The game began and ended with touches from van Persie but his team was not quite good enough to win the trophy. The stage was there for him to become an immortal but van Persie and his team were unable to take that chance. One cameraman must have known his match-winning potential and headed past the other players and straight for van Persie at full time – beaming pictures of the tired and distraught figure bending down in the centre circle, trying to come to terms with what had just happened.

Cesc Fàbregas, who had just won the World Cup for the first time in his country's history, showed great compassion when he ran over to console club mate van Persie. He said: 'The first thing I did was go to Robin. I had to go to him instead of celebrating with my friends. It is really hard for him. He has been injured for a long time. Of course, if it wasn't Spain he was playing against I would have been on his side.

'Even though I was really happy I was sad for him because he deserves it as well. He just said congratulations and told me to enjoy the moment. He is a great guy, a great leader but has been really unlucky with injuries. I really hope he can have his moment next year, or in two or four years, and that he can win something.'

That meeting encapsulated the togetherness of the Arsenal squad but Fàbregas' words came as most fans were resigned to losing the midfielder to the club where he learned his craft – Barcelona. It seemed his heart belonged to the Catalan club but they went on to have a £40 million bid turned down and the two, who clearly cared deeply about each other, would have the opportunity to turn their bond into success. Maybe even a long-awaited trophy was finally on the cards for the longing shelves of the North London club's bare trophy cabinet.

It was unsurprising that van Persie found something to moan about with the bitter taste of defeat in his mouth. Referee Howard Webb came in for criticism for 'three big errors' van Persie thinks changed the game. He asked: 'What was this man doing? He made three big errors in extra time of a final and believe me, this really hurts. Even after Heitinga's red card I still felt we could be world champions. With penalty kicks we'd at least have a 50 per cent chance. Iniesta should not have been on the pitch because he kicked van Bommel. He also should have shown Carles Puyol a second yellow card for trying to knock down Arjen Robben. The referee has been decisive.'

A lot of post-match analysis quite rightly asked why the Netherlands played in such a well-measured, at times restrained, at times aggressive manner. Surely this was not the way the national team was meant to play – whatever happened to them playing some of the most beautiful football in the world?

When van Marwijk had taken over the reins in 2008, he said the team would 'learn how to defend' but nobody really took any notice as they strolled their way to maximum points in an extremely successful qualification campaign. The point being made was that perhaps the Netherlands were more likely to win if they abandoned their traditional style of play.

Van Persie told the *Mail on Sunday*: 'It was not as pretty as it used to be with Holland and people criticised us for our playing style. But my question is: Getting results and reaching the final or playing the beautiful game and getting knocked out in the first round – which would you choose?

'Just before France had to pack their bags, Patrick Vieira said to me that you don't have to play well in the group stages of a World Cup, not even in the second round. Only later do you have to grow as a team and you will reach a high level. That will get you to the final. That is exactly the way we did it. Against Brazil in the second half, we were brilliant.'

Van Persie reasoned that Arsenal's five years without winning a trophy proved his point perfectly. Wenger had assembled a team famed for playing beautiful football that would always find its match somewhere along the line. 'I know how difficult it can be to play wonderful football and not get the result you want,' he said. 'I see it at Arsenal more than I want to. When we play the likes of Bolton and Blackburn we dominate the game, we play attacking football and they score from a lousy throw-in or an odd corner-kick. Then we end up chasing them again. The criticism Holland got in the World Cup I recognise from what we get at Arsenal. It was a final. You don't give up without a fight, do you?'

Maybe Arsène Wenger needed to sit up and take note. Van Persie had a fair point about those Blackburn and Bolton set-pieces. Perhaps the lesson to be learned from van Persie's 2010 World Cup exploits was that everything has its time and place. Sometimes a team needs to battle and grind out a result and at other times that bit of 'va-va-voom' magic can win a game.

A one-trick pony can never aspire to much. In his years at Highbury and The Emirates, van Persie had seen Arsenal play beautiful football but at times allow themselves to be kicked off the field. Van Marwijk's Netherlands were more like a hybrid side – a strong backbone with a mean attitude but with a couple of special players to turn on the style when the situation allowed.

When he'd come up against Italy star Francesco Totti in the World Cup group stages, van Persie had initially thought he was a 'hugely arrogant' person. That viewpoint changed when he discovered the star gives away 75 per cent of his salary to charity. Totti's generosity with time and money to good causes was something van Persie had in common with the enigmatic AS Roma attacker.

Robin and his wife had been donating money to the SOS Children campaign after Bouchra had met a struggling family whilst in Kenya. After initially agreeing to sponsor three-year-old Nelly, they later decided it would be more appropriate to sponsor the whole family that included a total of 10 children.

Van Persie told the *Mirror* he had enjoyed a special bond with African players over the years and was aware of the struggles people faced in some countries. He said: 'Ever since I was a young player I have always been friends with African players, so I know all about life out there. At Arsenal, there is Alex Song, Emmanuel Eboué and Kolo Touré. All those guys are my friends.'

After showing true heart to lend support to that African family, Bouchra joined forces with the partners of Cesc Fàbregas and Thomas Vermaelen to organise a charity event to promote SOS Children's Villages. The fundraising trio arranged a lavish event at London's famous Claridge's hotel at the start of December.

Robin was proud of the hard work put in by his other half and said: 'I've been in other charities but the amount of time they have put in, starting at nine in the morning, finishing at one, at midnight, has been amazing.'

The ladies of Arsenal were setting a fine example by putting their fame and connections to good use. Wives and girlfriends of footballers had a reputation for being self-centred and out of touch with reality, so it was great to see Bouchra break the mould. She was not in the relationship just to reap the benefits of dating a Premier League star – the pair were childhood sweethearts. This maybe made her likelier to be grateful for what she had and therefore more likely to be charitable.

Arsenal Football Club had always been a great champion of good causes and had a nominated charity each year that they strived to raise funds for. When the side played Fulham in December 2010, Robin and the rest of the Arsenal players donated a day's wages to Centrepoint – London's biggest youth-focused homelessness charity. Despite developing a bad reputation by filling newspaper gossip columns, many top footballers had displayed generosity and kindness. The 'Team England Footballers Charity' has seen players donate their wages to charity for several years.

With Arsenal's championing of charities, it is unsurprising that prestigious names connected with the club had seized the initiative and begun spearheading their own campaigns. Sol Campbell set up 'Kids Go Live', a charity that aimed to give inner city youngsters the chance to watch prestigious live sports matches. Towering centre back Campbell believed it was important that high-profile sporting events were accessible to all children, not just those from affluent areas. Thierry Henry supported the Cystic Fibrosis Trust and UNICEF for many years whilst David Seaman enthusiastically promoted the humorously named annual 'Safe Hands' charity golf event to raise money for Cancer Research UK.

It wasn't just Bouchra who was keen to get behind good causes, as Robin put his weight behind the BBC's Sport Relief by posing for promotional photographs and encouraging fans to get involved. Before too long he was also at the centre of a Teenage Cancer Trust campaign conducted by Arsenal.

Those were far from isolated incidents for van Persie as he went on to back a string of charity events. The 27-year-old was challenged to draw a self-portrait as part of a fundraiser for the Nordoff Robbins charity. Despite later admitting that as a child he felt he did not have the talent to live up to his parents' artistic expectations, van Persie was confident enough to draw himself for charity. His effort drew comparisons to van Persie's contributions on the field as he had made a positive contribution whilst thinking creatively. The work of art certainly drew on the skills inherited from his arty parents.

Graphologist Emma Bache analysed the picture to see what could be told about van Persie from the image he had created of himself. She said: 'Robin's picture is a caricature and what is most striking is the very large eyes, so he's an observer and a genuine person. There's a broad grin there which suggests he's honest, open and has nothing to hide. The sparse hair shows speed, but also a sense of humour and a large character. The signature, written at an angle, has a rigidity that suggests his feelings and thoughts aren't swayed by others but also that he has very strong values. The writing goes small after the capital letters which shows he doesn't have a very big ego.'

This was a pretty much spot-on reflection of van Persie's character, maybe minus the ego. That venture into art had been so enjoyable that a couple of years later he persuaded Tomáš Rosický to pick up a brush as the pair had pieces auctioned off for the Willow Foundation.

The couple were enthusiastic backers of a number of good causes but they had the humility to stop well short of parading around kissing babies on the forehead. It was heartening to spot the couple swimming against the tide in the sea of selfishness that was modern football.

After coming so close in South Africa, van Persie returned to England with renewed optimism. He might not have been able to lift the World Cup trophy this time around but, as was said at the start of every season, he had a realistic chance of winning the Premier League with Arsenal. They hadn't won the title since 2004 but in Wenger they had a manager who had already led them to England's greatest prize on three previous occasions.

After the Netherlands' slightly unattractive brand of football had nearly seen the team win the World Cup, van Persie had remarked that Arsenal needed to get tougher and that there was no point playing brilliantly only to cancel their good work out by giving simplistic goals away and being muscled out of contention.

When he was back in England preparing for the 2010/2011 season, van Persie soon ditched talk of a tougher Arsenal and instead chose to compare the team to one of the best sides in club football – Barcelona. He told the club's website: 'I love the way of thinking at Arsenal, the way of playing really stands out. I know two teams who play similar football; they are us and Barcelona. Some teams are trying but not really coming close.

Their play had not always been quite up to Barcelona's when the two sides had met in the past but van Persie's heart was in the right place. It was true that he had played alongside players from clubs with a variety of footballing philosophies whilst on Netherlands duty. This is part of how playing international football improves a player because van Persie had found himself in the same team as footballers who were used to playing in completely different ways. Even if he did not agree with those styles and they were not the way Arsène Wenger would want him to play, the fact that he had thought about them made him better prepared to play against teams using that footballing approach in the future.

He continued: 'I speak to colleagues in the national team

from different big teams which have a different way of thinking. But I prefer our way of thinking, very much. That's why I believe and I don't stop believing when things go against us. I have never stopped believing in Arsenal. I love this club, this is my seventh year now. Arsenal gave me a chance to develop into a good player and I want to repay the club and the fans and everyone with trophies.'

Repaying those fans with trophies was a much more realistic proposition than in past seasons as Arsène Wenger's talented squad was coming of age whereas their rivals' progress appeared to be stalling. Reigning champions Chelsea and red-hot title contenders Manchester United had not made many major improvements to their squads much since the 2009/2010 season and Arsenal's youngsters were growing up – plus they had managed to keep hold of want-away star Fàbregas. Chelsea's John Terry and United's Wayne Rooney – each arguably their club's most highly regarded and influential player – were both still reeling from newspaper revelations that they had cheated on their wives.

As the season began, Arsenal had a togetherness the other clubs would have envied. Even if a tabloid revelation had upset the form of one of their players, Arsenal would have been in a better position to carry on than their rivals because they were a tightly-knit team unit without a 'star man' who was more important than his colleagues.

When Thierry Henry, whom supporters voted the best player in Arsenal's history on the club's website, left the club in 2007, Wenger received an ear-bashing for not bringing in another 'big name' player. The manager clearly knew what he was doing and maybe it would eventually serve to make the club stronger in the long run. It is possible to set up a team to stifle one player you think will present a stand-alone threat but it becomes pretty difficult when facing a team that does not have one obvious area to suppress.

Before the 2010 season got underway, Arsenal turned down a £40 million bid from Barcelona for Cesc Fàbregas. Some felt this handed Fàbregas the 'star man' mantle at the Emirates and this might have unsettled van Persie a bit. Fàbregas had moved to Highbury eight months before van Persie signed from Feyenoord and had always seemed to have one up on the Dutchman – Fàbregas is four years younger than van Persie, has acted as Arsenal's captain with van Persie as vice-captain and of course he set up Iniesta's goal that beat van Persie and the Netherlands 1-0 in that final in Johannesburg.

Wenger took the sensible decision to ease his World Cup stars back into the team and not push them straight into pre-season friendly action. Van Persie did not get on the pitch during Arsenal's pre-season campaign but came off the bench on the opening afternoon of the Premier League season. With 15 minutes remaining as Arsenal trailed 1-0 at Liverpool, who had had new signing Joe Cole sent off, both managers flexed their muscles as Liverpool's World Cup winner Fernando Torres (who had, on a personal level at least, endured an even more frustrating tournament than van Persie) joined the field at the same time as van Persie.

He may not have quite had the measure of the Jabulani ball in South Africa but van Persie's team mates knew he was more than capable with the Premier League's more familiar Nike ball. Van Persie pumped two corners into the box to create mayhem but when it finally fell to Walcott, he fired over.

Arsenal were pushing for an equaliser against Liverpool's 10 men but Pepe Reina was playing a blinder between the sticks for the home side. Tomáš Rosický, Marouane Chamakh and Theo Walcott all went close as it looked like it wasn't to be the Gunners' day. The equaliser eventually did come in the last minute when Chamakh beat Reina to a cross, which bounced off the post, hit the keeper and rolled into the net.

If Arsenal were to turn the polite respect their football commanded into trophies, it was now or never. They needed the likes of van Persie to find their form and younger players like Theo Walcott and Samir Nasri to show they had become men.

Wenger didn't feel van Persie was fully fit so kept him on the bench when Ian Holloway's Blackpool visited the Emirates the following week. Arsenal were already five goals to the good when van Persie and Fàbregas were brought on with an hour played. Notably there was a warmer reception for the Spaniard, with fans relieved to see him somehow not join Barcelona. It is a safe bet that van Persie would have been envious of the cheering crowd holding banners proclaiming their love for Fàbregas but he did his best to carry on.

Unlike at Anfield the previous week, Arsenal were completely on top against the unfancied Blackpool and if it weren't for the heroics of goalkeeper Matthew Gilks it could easily have been double figures. After nice interplay with emerging star Jack Wilshere, van Persie whipped in a delightful ball for 'King Cesc', who was unable to connect.

Hearts were in mouths when van Persie, with heavy strapping on his thighs, went down injured and had to leave the field for treatment. He returned a minute later seemingly unaffected and volleyed narrowly wide as Arsenal looked to bump up their goal difference. As was the story in the World Cup, van Persie may not have been on the score sheet but he was racking up the assists. As the game drew to a close his accurate corner (and Blackpool's poor marking) did all the work for Marouane Chamakh as the Morocco international headed past Gilks from the penalty spot. Van Persie tried his luck in injury time but he shot straight at the goalkeeper.

Something worrying on a personal level for van Persie was post-match talk that Walcott, who starred with a hat-trick, could move in from his usual position on the wing to become a more effective force up front. This was competition for places that van Persie did not need – especially as Walcott would be a lot sharper, having not been selected by Fabio Capello for England's disastrous World Cup campaign. He would need to show the world what he was about in the match at Blackburn or risk being forgotten about.

The game at Ewood Park was van Persie's first start of the season, giving a real opportunity to make his mark. An early touch should have settled him down but when Blackburn players started snapping away at those delicate ankles, van Persie would have felt more uncomfortable than he had earlier in the day.

Two minutes in, Fàbregas was caught in possession and laid the ball off to van Persie. Once again he has hassled out of possession and was looking a bit off the pace. His body might not have been quite up to pace but that creative brain was still ticking away. In a similar way that aging stars drop down a few leagues and still manage to dictate play – 36-year old Darren Anderton turning out for AFC Bournemouth in League Two springs to mind – van Persie was making measured passes and intelligently flicking the ball around the field but always late on the scene.

Christopher Samba should have given Blackburn the lead when slack marking at a corner kick from van Persie presented him with a free header. The Dutchman was nowhere near the ball and extremely fortunate the 6-foot 4 Republic of Congo defender was unable to keep his header down.

In the 20th minute van Persie finally hit his stride when he found a bit of pace to create space and spot Theo Walcott on the right-hand side. His inch-perfect pass put last week's hat-trick hero through to slide home the opening goal. The well-measured ball was expertly controlled and dispatched by the 21-year-old, who was motoring ahead of van Persie in the goalscoring stakes. It was all about van Persie's pass and his team mates let him know how important his contribution was by mobbing van Persie rather than Walcott as the pair ran off to celebrate.

Van Persie's tail was up and the travelling supporters were chanting his name as he prepared to swing in a corner. However things started to go wrong as the game approached the half-hour mark. First Mame Diouf made it 1-1 and then van Persie suffered a fresh injury blow, which was of his own making. After coming under pressure from Ryan Nelson, he lost control of the ball and Phil Jones looked set to win possession back for Blackburn. Van Persie panicked and as the 18-year-old hacked the ball away from danger, van Persie led with his left foot – studs in the air –

as he tried to block. Had Jones chosen to make a meal of the collision or referee Chris Foy seen what had happened, surely a dismissal was on the cards. It was a horror tackle that could have seen Jones' leg snapped in the same way Eduardo's had been snapped by Birmingham's Martin Taylor two seasons previously.

It had passed unnoticed because Jones was unhurt and van Persie was injured, but this was the sort of thing expected of a Sunday league pub team player, not a highly-paid white-booted football machine. Every player has a downside to their game and it appeared van Persie's was this 'dark side' that saw him lunging in whilst chasing lost causes – as he had done to kick-start the shower of yellow cards in the World Cup final, and indeed for that red card at Southampton back in 2005.

It had always been Arsène Wenger's trademark to make complaints about his players being victimised and targeted by the bigger, more physical teams such as Blackburn but van Persie had shown Arsenal were as guilty as anybody of unruly behaviour. Van Persie could have done his reputation a lot of damage if that challenge had connected.

It was a slightly scaled-down version of the infamous 1991 FA Cup final incident in which a wild Paul Gascoigne lunge saw him obtain a serious cruciate ligament injury. Van Persie fell straight to the ground and needed treatment to that left ankle. He carried on for a couple of minutes but was not able to run and walked around the pitch clearly in a lot of pain. He was off the pace as it was and this just made things ridiculous – it looked like he needed a walking stick. Minutes later he was on the floor again, grimacing in pain and holding that left ankle. Marouane Chamakh came on to replace him in the 35th minute and van Persie cut a forlorn figure as he limped off the pitch.

Fans of most teams believe their club has an 'injury curse' and Arsenal supporters are no different. After Andrey Arshavin had won the game for the Gunners, talk immediately switched to the fact that van Persie was once again on the treatment table. Gunners fans moaned that he had been able to complete a World Cup tournament without injury problems yet he picked up an injury on his first start of the season for Arsenal. Scans showed he had damaged the left ankle (it was his right ankle that had kept him out for five months of the previous season) and would be out for three weeks or more.

Arsène Wenger didn't seem overly concerned about this latest setback and said it was just a twisted ankle that would heal in around 18 days, but it had to be a concern that injuries were affecting the same part of his body. In the long term, repeated knocks to van Persie's ankles might seriously limit his ability to play and could even cut his career short.

It was extremely frustrating for van Persie as the Dutch Football Association announced he would definitely miss both of their opening Euro 2012 qualifying matches. In six seasons with the Gunners van Persie was yet to make 100 Premier League starts, but with nearly 50 league goals to his name, he was far too valuable to toss into the bin. Any talk of him having more success in a less physical league – say for example Spain's La Liga – was nullified by the fact that the injury was self-inflicted. If he was going to fly around with high studs, the injuries would keep on coming. That spell on the sidelines would prove to be longer than was initially predicted as van Persie did not see any action for the whole of September and October.

On Sunday 7 November, the crowd roared as van Persie was back in action. With Arsenal trailing 1-0 at home to Newcastle, whose special plan to stage an Andy Carroll-led assault on the delicate Arsenal defence was working a treat. Marouane Chamakh was hauled off and the Dutchman bounced onto the pitch to a great reception from the Emirates crowd. However it was not to be a happy return as Carroll – in the sort of form that would earn him an England call-up later that month – proved the difference between the two sides with his powerful first-half header.

While he was an unused substitute for Arsenal's next few matches, it came as something of a shock when it was announced van Persie had been named in the Dutch squad for their friendly with Turkey on 17 November. It perfectly summed up the unconventional route van Persie's career often takes that he had only played a matter of minutes for his club and was already back in the international fold. It also spelled out loud and clear just how highly rated he is with national coach van Marwijk.

His club manager Arsène Wenger was initially perplexed by the call-up and said it was a 'surreal' thing to happen. FIFA rules prevented him from standing in van Persie's way. He dejectedly told a press conference: 'The situation is a bit surreal because he hasn't played for us. All the rest is down to the rules for international games. What can I do about that? Not a lot.'

Van Persie came on in the second half and set up Rafael van der Vaart with a well-measured through-ball from which the Tottenham man really should have scored.

Klaas-Jan Huntelaar scored the only goal of the game as the Netherlands won 1-0, with van Persie a little off the pace – he was absent for the move which led to the goal and missed most of the resulting celebration as he was clearly struggling for pace.

After being brought on at half-time in the 1-0 win in Amsterdam, van Persie was keen to play down the controversy involved in his selection: 'I see it as a win-win situation. I am pleased that the Dutch coach is happy and that the coach of Arsenal is also happy. It all went well. I was not troubled by the match, everything went according to plan. The training that I've had with the Dutch team, I have not had at Arsenal.'

After being given a few days to rest, van Persie was given more game time by his club in the League Cup quarter-final game at home to Wigan Athletic three days later. The fact that the games were coming thick and fast for Arsenal in the notoriously busy Christmas period afforded van Persie more opportunity for game time than he might have otherwise been allowed.

The League Cup usually comes low in the priority of title-challenging clubs and Arsène Wenger has used the competition to give a lot of youngsters a piece of first-team action. Indeed Arsenal have only won the competition twice in their history – in 1987 and 1993. But, as Bob Dylan said, times they are a-changing.

After fielding teams full of first-choice players for their games against Tottenham and Newcastle in previous rounds, Wenger agreed that he was taking the competition more seriously in the 2010/2011 season than ever before. He said: 'I have many players who are top level and I have many players who are young as well. We will play a team with a good chance to win the game because we want to qualify. Knowing how the Premier League is now, one advantage as a manager is you do not have to warn your team because everybody knows how difficult it is.'

Thanks to hugely discounted ticket prices – £10 for adults when usually the cheapest seats at the Emirates start at around the £35 mark – nearly 60,000 people crammed into the ground to watch van Persie start the game as captain. He might not have hit the back of the net but the number 10 played a pivotal role in Arsenal's win.

This was his first start since August but it was a commanding performance. Midway through the first half Wilshere played the ball to van Persie, who had his back to goal. Before the Wigan defence had time to gather themselves, a sublime back-heel fed Carlos Vela who shot narrowly wide. Wigan's Maynor Figueroa was lucky not to concede a penalty when he appeared to handle with van Persie lurking at the back stick. Arsenal had been unable to score but Antolin Alcaraz kindly headed into his own net to give the home side the lead on the stroke of half-time.

In the second half van Persie was a bit quieter after his attempt to win a header saw him floored by a knock to the nose. He was substituted to a round of applause with 15 minutes remaining. He did not quite get on the score sheet but this was a brilliant comeback game and it was only fitting that supporters voted their returning superstar man of the match on the club's official website after the game.

Arsène Wenger was understandably delighted to see his star man returning to full fitness. After the game he said: 'Van Persie is getting stronger every day. He had 70 minutes against Wigan and I am confident that if we can get him injury free he will be back to his best level.'

It was no coincidence that with this return to the fold, Arsenal made their way back to the top of the Premier League table. On Saturday 4 December van Persie changed the game after coming on as a substitute with an hour left with the Gunners and Fulham drawing one apiece. Twelve minutes and a few deft touches later and Samir Nasri had been put through by our man to score and seal the win that took Arsenal to the top of the Premier League for the first time in months.

After making his return, van Persie soon found himself making a first Champions League start of the season. He didn't take long to get the ball rolling by winning and scoring a penalty as Arsenal went on to beat Partizan Belgrade 3-1. A win was vital if the Gunners wanted to qualify from a challenging Group H, where they were not given the easy ride some fans may have expected them to receive.

Resisting the 'look of 2010' snood, which certain other 'trendy' team mates opted for, he came in to captain the side and sat in the hole behind Chamakh. Van Persie spent a lot of the game around the edge of the box acting as the pivot around which the Gunners' moves were constructed.

The Serbians were whipping boys of Group H but held out for half an hour before a sprinkling of Dutch magic prised them open. Alex Song delicately flicked the ball into van Persie's path and as he jinked through, Marko Jovanovic could not deal with his injection of pace and brought him down for a penalty. Wearing the captain's armband, van Persie led by example and smashed the spot-kick into the top right-hand corner of the net. It was so nearly two for the captain later when his free-kick was flipped over the bar by Vladimir Stojkovic. It says something about the quality of the man that he was able to come in and play such an integral part in this victory despite only having made two previous starts.

When interviewed by ITV in their post-match analysis, van Persie was clearly brimming with confidence. Asked if the team believed they could win the competition, he said: 'We have to. Everything starts with belief. If you don't have belief you'd better stop playing football. We do believe. The pressure was on today and they played quite well. Partizan are a good side, they kept the ball quite well. We had to run a lot.'

Wenger was thrilled with van Persie's impressive showing despite the fact that he was not still quite up to 100 per cent. Wenger said: 'It's important that he comes back to a good fitness level. I think he became stronger and stronger during the game.'

That was praise indeed as Wenger justified his decision to hand the captain's armband to a man nowhere near his best. After he opened the scoring and brilliantly set up Samir Nasri's goal later in the game, there was still criticism of van Persie amongst Arsenal supporters. There were claims on online fans' forums that he was selfish and needed to set up his team mates rather than opting to shoot all the time.

There was heated debate about whether placing him behind Chamakh – who failed to score – was a good idea. These forums aren't always a hotbed of reasoned debate but perhaps they were right – van Persie did appear to be going for the spectacular and neglecting the realistic. When you consider he had only just returned to the side and had been made captain, it is little wonder that he was eager to impress.

Wenger, who had been Arsenal manager for over 14 years at the time of this dispute, knew how quickly this kind of situation could have escalated if he were to say nothing about it. He swiftly moved to end speculation that van Persie and Chamakh, who joined from Bordeaux in a free transfer in May 2010, would not work well alongside each other. He told the club's official website: 'We can play Chamakh and van Persie together. We can play Chamakh up front and van Persie behind. What is interesting is that we can play all kinds of formations with the two.'

Van Persie got 2011 off to a bang when he scored his 75th Arsenal goal in a 3-0 victory over Birmingham City at St Andrews. The signs were good for the New Year when van Persie used a couple of early free-kicks to find his range. Those sighters paid off when he smashed a free-kick past Ben Foster with only 13 minutes played of the team's first match of the year. Nasri netted a second after being found in a great position by van Persie before Roger Johnson finished off by scoring an own goal. Van Persie told Sky Sports that he was impressed with the result and said that Arsenal's quality play had been rewarded with some 'good goals'. There were suggestions he had dived to win the free-kick from which he hit the first goal of the evening. He insisted: 'There was contact before the moment and that was why I was out of balance. When I went down it was a clear free-kick in my opinion.'

Arsène Wenger said Arsenal had done well in a physical game and that his team looked calm. He insisted that if they kept faith in the way they played, Arsenal would be a success for years to come. Questions were still being asked about whether Wenger's team of wonder-kids was actually capable of winning anything. Indeed, van Persie had only won the Charity Shield and FA Cup with the club and was itching to get his hands on more silverware with his thirtieth birthday not too far around the bend.

Considering the multitude of injury problems he had to contend with, 75 goals from 145 starts had been a good haul for Arsenal and provided a solid platform for him to build on. Continuing his good work in the next few years could well see van Persie score as many goals as Dennis Bergkamp or make as many appearances as Edwin van der Sar. If he could finally have a period undisrupted by fitness problems, van Persie would surely be in line to claim honours for both club and country with a long period of his playing career still ahead of him. His hunger was there, his commitment was there and his skill was there. The only thing missing was a major trophy.

CHAPTER 8

BREAKTHROUGH MOVE

Despite starting 2011 in a commanding position, come the summer Arsenal's trophy drought was extended by another season. After being within a point of leaders Manchester United at the end of February, they tumbled to a final Premier League finish of fourth place. After once again being dumped out of the Champions League by Barcelona, Wenger's men somehow managed to lose the League Cup final to Birmingham City, who would go on to be relegated from the top flight a few months later.

The magic of Robin van Persie was there for all to see when he sneakily worked an inch of ground in the penalty area and volleyed home a glorious equaliser in that Wembley defeat to Birmingham. Unfortunately, the luck of Robin van Persie was also on show as he picked up a knee problem while scoring the goal, an injury that not only meant the

THE BIOGRAPHY OF ROBIN VAN PERSIE

captain missed the rest of that ill-fated final but also made him unavailable at a crucial time of the season. Then, upon his return to fitness, van Persie was harshly sent off for a second yellow card offence in Arsenal's 3-1 defeat at the Nou Camp, after taking a shot when the referee had blown his whistle to stop the game. Despite all his poor fortune, the Dutchman still topped his club's scoring charts, notching an impressive 18 goals in just 25 league appearances.

Those injury worries were put firmly behind van Persie in the 2011/12 season, as he made a total of 48 appearances for the club in all competitions. After notching his 100th goal for the club in September, Robin hit seven goals in just five games in October, acting like a faithful dog pulling its drowning owner to the surface of a muddy lake by the scruff of the neck. By February he had surpassed Denis Bergkamp's 120-goal Arsenal haul, and was single-handedly keeping the club in contention for a Champions League qualifying finish.

Despite Robin's best efforts, his team mates were simply not cutting the mustard and it would prove to be a trophy-less season, and the Gunners left it late to secure a spot in the Champions League for the following season.

At the end of the campaign, Arsenal's top goalscorer chart (all competitions) read as follows: Yossi Benayoun (6), Theo Walcott (11), Robin van Persie (37). There it is in black and white: he carried the team. Calls were made for Wenger's head and Arsenal fans were petrified their one standout player would consider jumping ship to be a realistic option. Why wouldn't he?

With 30 Premier League goals, van Persie was the top goalscorer in arguably the world's toughest league. Both the

PFA (Professional Footballers' Association) and the FWA (Football Writers' Association) named the Dutchman as their player of the year. With just a year remaining on his contract, under the Bosman ruling, the following summer he would be free to walk into the arms of another club without a chequebook being so much as fished from a pocket.

Contract negotiations were put back until van Persie returned from the impending European Championship tournament, where he would be one of the figureheads of the Dutch side. To their credit, Arsenal acted fast before van Persie returned for talks, snapping up forwards Lukas Podolski and Olivier Giroud. The critically acclaimed pair not only bolstered the squad but also signalled the club's intent to do better in the next campaign. A three-pronged attack was mentioned and Wenger spoke of the new recruits' unselfishness.

The Netherlands were among the favourites for the 2012 European Championship, staged in Poland and Ukraine. After winning nine out of ten qualifying matches to make the tournament, both van Persie and the team approached the group stages in menacing form. Van Persie did score an absolute screamer – a right-footed 25-yarder against Germany – but that was a rare highlight in a disastrous tournament for the Oranje. Bert Van Marwijk's men were humbled by a somewhat ordinary Denmark side in their opening group game and never really recovered.

That wonder-goal against eventual semi-finalists Germany proved a mere consolation in a 2-1 defeat, while Cristiano Ronaldo's brace for Portugal in the final group game made it a clean sweep of defeats for a team that had come so close to winning the World Cup just two years earlier. It was the first time the Netherlands had lost three competitive games on the spin and van Marwijk resigned soon afterwards to draw a line in the sand.

Despite a below-par showing in Poland and Ukraine, Robin van Persie remained hot property in the 2012 summer transfer window. Other clubs knew the Arsenal board would be under pressure to cash in on Robin while they could, or face the wrath of supporters if he walked away for nothing in the summer of 2013 under the Bosman rule. Sol Campbell audaciously moved to Arsenal from bitter rivals Spurs in 2001 and supporters were scared stiff that a star player could do the same thing to their own club one day.

For Arsenal to lose one of their most valuable players of the modern era for nothing would be unthinkable; yet if a contract was not signed over the summer, that would become a distinct possibility. Every club in the world knew that, and surely some would chance their arm with a bid. So while Wenger insisted the Gunners should cling on to their iconic number 10 at all costs, the likes of Manchester City and Juventus circled above the Emirates, claws outstretched.

Van Persie was firmly in the driving seat: he could choose to stay with Arsenal or join the reigning English or Italian champions. Even more avenues would surely open up if he publicly stated a desire to move. While in one sense it must be great to be the most important player in the team, it must have been an incredibly frustrating few years for van Persie, whose performances deserved those trophies and medals that the shortcomings of his team mates denied him.

Whatever badge Robin would wear on his shirt in the next few seasons, he would only have half a decade or so at the peak of his powers before time would begin to take a toll on that 6-foot 1 frame. At the age of 29 and with not a lot of silverware to show for his immense talent, would Robin van Persie end up as one of the biggest unfulfilled talents in the history of the modern game?

There were also rumours through the summer that Manchester United were interested in capturing van Persie. With rivals City reigning Premier League champions and looking to strengthen and defend their crown, United's legendary manager Sir Alex Ferguson kept it old school and picked up the phone to have a chat with Arsène Wenger.

Wenger said the series of conversations between English football's two longest serving managers were of a professional nature; the pair had clashed in the past but also had a great deal of respect for each other. The outcome of the telephone exchange was that Robin van Persie joined Manchester United for £24 million.

The Arsenal ship is a very tight one and the prospect of losing their best player for nothing would have kept a few of the men upstairs awake at night. They decided to cash in when the chance presented itself and the sale was agreed. United were rumoured to be paying a £250,000-a-week wage – double what any player earn at The Emirates; but it was the chance to win major honours that really pushed him to move.

Wenger later bizarrely compared van Persie to a woman who was about to turn 40 and was desperate to have a child. He told a press conference: 'She starts to think, "I have no time left!"' Despite the somewhat bizarre analogy, the Frenchman was right that van Persie had decided it was 'now or never': he had to move in order to secure a trophy.

Sir Alex Ferguson brought some of the best players to Manchester United for extremely moderate fees: Peter Schmeichel joined for £500,000, Eric Cantona was £1.2 million and Teddy Sheringham cost just £3.5 million from Tottenham. Of the four players who had joined for a higher transfer fee than van Persie, two of them failed to set the world alight – Fergie would have cursed his luck after splashing out the best part of £60 million on Juan Sebastian Veron and Dimitar Berbatov.

But he had broken the £20 million barrier to sign the English top flight's hottest property in the past – Rio Ferdinand and Wayne Rooney both went on to become legends at the club. Would van Persie follow in Ferdinand's footsteps or flop like Argentinian Veron?

Things did not get off to a promising start. After being pipped to the title by City in injury time at the end of the 2011/2012 season, United were looking to start the season with a bang. His new team kicked things off with a 1-0 defeat at Everton; as van Persie came off the bench for his first appearance, David Moyes' men bossed throughout and were good value for their win. Clearly this was not going to be the instant success that had been billed.

Journalists licked their lips and began to type the 'c' word – crisis – as Damien Duff slipped in to give Fulham a third-minute lead at Old Trafford in the next match. Van Persie started this game, however, and was given a chance to level matters with 10 minutes gone when Patrice Evra crossed from the right; his sweet finish into the opposite corner of the net was a sign of true class as the striker waited for the ball to bounce and sit up before striking. Many would have snatched early at the chance, but a true predator has a calm head and strikes at the right time. He later told BBC Sport that he was not thinking too much and just hit it; it was a very natural strike that was a sign of true class.

An eventual 3-2 win kick-started the side's campaign but this was one of those afternoons where the scoreline is overshadowed by other events. As substitute Rooney blocked a Fulham cross, Hugo Rodallega landed on top of him and the England man's thigh was nastily gashed. With Rooney on the sidelines for at least a month, van Persie had a chance to cement a starting place in the side and show his new team mates and supporters how valuable he could be.

What better way to do so than to score a hat-trick in your next game? United were again below par as van Persie's two late goals turned a 2-1 deficit into victory at Southampton. Somewhere in the middle of all that he had a chipped penalty patted away, but in the end that did not matter. It was a red letter afternoon as Sir Alex Ferguson celebrated 1,000 matches in charge of Manchester United and the Dutchman notched his 100th career Premier League goal. It was reminiscent of the tail end of his Arsenal career as van Persie led from the front, dragging his team mates over the line. His first goal was a wonderful back-to-basics volley, while the winning header in injury time sparked wild scenes in the St Mary's away end.

A goal for the Netherlands in a routine 2-0 World Cup qualifying win over Turkey made it five strikes in van Persie's last four matches as he refused to take his foot off the gas. His new employers continued to purr as van Persie stroked home a penalty 10 minutes from time to seal a 2-1 win over Liverpool at Anfield. That miss on the south coast could have played on his mind but the Dutchman kept his nerve to bag maximum points for the team; he had learned to stand strong under the weight of expectation.

With nine goals in his first twelve run-outs for United, the memory of that jilted former lover was starting to fade into the distance. But just as Old Trafford was starting to feel like home, Arsenal rolled into town. Most of the Gunners squad had played with van Persie, which should have given them an advantage.

It emerged before the game that when the pair were negotiating in the summer, Wenger had told Ferguson: 'He's better than you think.' Mind games were a common occurrence between the pair: was this an attempt at reverse psychology? It mattered not: after the travelling Arsenal fans gave him a less than welcoming reception, van Persie responded by finding the net with just three minutes played to set the hosts on their way to another three points.

Defeat left the north Londoners down in sixth place, with United a point clear at the top of the Premier League table with 10 games played. There was a long way to go but with a quarter of the season played, that switch of allegiances looked a shrewd move. When he was given a choice of squad numbers at the start of the season, van Persie chose to wear number 20 because United were going for a record 20th English top flight title; this dream was well on its way to becoming a reality.

The Christmas and New Year period can often be when a title challenge falls away, or when champions motor on and put themselves in a commanding position. After their defeat at Norwich in November, United went undefeated until March, when the might of a certain Cristiano Ronaldo and his Real Madrid colleagues brought their Champions League campaign to an abrupt halt. Central to that success was the star striker, who went on a run of 10 goals in 10 league games.

On their way to the title in the previous season, Roberto Mancini's side had left Old Trafford shell-shocked as they romped to a remarkable 6-1 victory. It was not quite so emphatic, but United set the record straight with a last-ditch 3-2 win at the Etihad in December. Rooney had put the red half of Manchester into a first half two-goal lead, but it looked like it would finish honours even as Pablo Zabaleta drew the hosts level just four minutes from time. But after Carlos Tevez sent Rafael tumbling to the floor, van Persie hit a deflected free-kick past Joe Hart to spark wild celebrations and send his side six points clear at the top of the table.

Mancini was spitting feathers after that 'unjust' defeat and he was pleased to restore pride with a 2-1 win at Old Trafford in April's return fixture. Sergio Agüero showed pace and a powerful finish to secure the bragging rights for the blue half of the city. That was all his side would have to show from the season, as United still finished the evening 12 points clear of them at the summit with just seven games left to play.

They were in this position despite the fact that van Persie had gone through a spell of just one goal in 10 games for his club. In his Arsenal days this would be unthinkable, but there was more back-up at Old Trafford: Javier Hernandez netted 10 Premier League goals that season and Wayne Rooney hit 12. Even the greatest strikers will go through a dry spell so it simply doesn't make sense to build a team around one main goalscoring threat.

He had the opportunity to finally bring a two-month goal drought to an end with a penalty kick on a freezing afternoon in Stoke. Michael Carrick had already put the visitors 1-0 up when Andy Wilkinson unceremoniously upended the Dutchman in the box. Stepping up to face Asmir Begovi , van Persie saw the ball blown off the penalty spot by a gust of wind as whistles and jeers from the notoriously raucous home fans grew louder. The ball was calmly replaced and lashed into the net, prompting an embrace with Ferguson in the dugout; the Scot later praised his composure and joked that: 'He forgets I'm 71 – he nearly killed me!'

After the match BBC Sport was told that it was all about the result and van Persie was not too bothered about ending his barren spell. Players feel obliged to say this; he would have been massively relieved to finally score.

The previous season's title race had gone right down to the wire but this time around things were much simpler. United were strolling home as they drew 2-2 at West Ham to inch closer to the title. Their rivals had a game in hand but faced a Spurs side with something still to play for – they were right on the tails of fourth-placed Chelsea and a Champions League spot. Andre Villas-Boas' men powered their way to a 3-1 win as Mancini conceded that his rivals deserved to win the title.

It was all set up: a win at home to struggling Aston Villa would seal a record 20th top-flight title for Manchester

United. In the build-up to the game Ferguson said he knew that van Persie could smell the finishing line: his time had finally come. Paul Lambert's men were in big trouble at the bottom of the table and United needed to be wary of the wounded beast: the proud club had won the European Cup just three decades ago but was now in danger of falling into the second tier. Old Trafford was packed out as United looked to make history in front of their own fans.

On such a landmark day, the 29-year-old needed to get himself a goal to ensure nobody came along to steal his glory. Welsh veteran Ryan Giggs made that a possibility when he redirected an Antonio Valencia cross right into van Persie's path two yards from goal with just 83 seconds played. It was on a plate for the Dutchman and he made no mistake from close range to put one hand onto the Premier League trophy.

Youthful Villa hadn't kept a clean sheet since January and it showed as the defence parted like the red sea. They had been thumped 8-0 by Chelsea earlier in the season and home fans licked their collective lips in anticipation of what might follow.

They were not given the cricket score some people might have been expecting, but everybody present saw a strike they would never forget. After 10 minutes of sitting back and soaking up Villa pressure, the home side seized control of the ball and looked to counter attack. According to Arsène Wenger, van Persie was injured less and scoring more because as the player matured, he learned to resist the temptation to track back when his side was not in possession. This was evident when Wayne Rooney emerged with the ball and began to make strides towards the halfway line.

He looked up and saw his fellow striker really high up the pitch, and instinctively chipped a Beckham-esque pass in his direction. Like a homing missile, van Persie continued his charge towards the penalty area and as the ball dropped over his right shoulder, took it on the volley first time with his left foot and used the pace of the ball to beat a bewildered Brad Guzan and send commentators scrambling for superlatives.

The likes of David Beckham, Ole Gunnar Solskjaer and Eric Cantona have all done amazing things in a red shirt, but Sir Alex Ferguson called van Persie's strike 'the goal of the century'. It was in the same league as – if not better than – that strike for Arsenal at Charlton seven years back, but this one also brought with it the importance of rubber-stamping a record-breaking title win.

Job done, so it would be easy to sit back and enjoy yourself a bit, right? Not this man: he pushed on and completed a triumphant 30-minute hat-trick, keeping his cool in the area to rifle into the roof of the net. Villa were beaten, van Persie had made his mark and the title was United's.

He had joined the right team at the right time and that long trophy drought was over. Winning the FA Cup is a wonderful moment in football but to lift the Premier League trophy means your team has performed well over the course of an entire season: a championship winning side is always a special one. He completed a lap of the pitch to celebrate delivering what was promised by that number 20 on the back of his shirt.

The title was won with four games left to play and it was written in the stars that the United bandwagon would roll into North London to face Arsenal in their next game. The

Gunners welcomed the champions onto the pitch at the Emirates with a guard of honour, which Wenger had urged supporters to observe with respect, but van Persie told a press conference beforehand that he expected a hostile welcome. There were some boos but also applause aplenty as van Persie and his men took to the field but he showed his former employers what they were missing by scoring a penalty as they dented Arsenal's push for a second-placed finish with a 1-1 draw. He chose not to celebrate but would have been smiling inside as his goal silenced those spitting vitriol at the 'deserter'.

It was a largely forgettable game with the take-away moment coming before a ball was even kicked as the stadium proved too familiar for the returning ace – he smiled and greeted former colleagues before nearly walking into the home dressing room. Suddenly he remembered where he needed to go, slapped himself on the forehead and walked into the away facilities with an embarrassed grin on his face.

In the week before the final home game of the season, which would see the team lift the Premier League trophy, Sir Alex Ferguson announced his retirement from football. He had reversed a retirement plan in 2002 but at the age of 71 finally his time was up. Including his brief spells at St Mirren and Aberdeen in Scotland, he had won an incredible 49 trophies as a manager. This would present a new challenge for van Persie, having spent years under the dependable leadership of mentor Arsène Wenger.

David Moyes, whose Everton team beat Ferguson's men on the opening day of the season, was set to come in as his replacement. He would have a new boss to impress and there were bound to be some changes in the summer.

The 2-1 win over Swansea was almost incidental on an emotional afternoon that saw the retirement of Sir Alex Ferguson and Paul Scholes. After collecting his medal, van Persie joked that the trophy was much heavier than he'd imagined. But with 26 Premier League goals in his debut season, he had earned the right to hold the trophy aloft.

He also took advantage of the opportunity to rub the triumph in Arsenal fan Piers Morgan's face; the former *News of the World* editor had labelled him a sell-out after switching clubs and tried to insult him by using the nickname 'van Pursestrings' – a reference to the huge increase in wages the Old Trafford switch brought with it. A package containing a signed photo of van Persie with the Premier League trophy was sent to Piers' Beverly Hills address. The chat show host took the joke well and announced that he was going to keep the picture in his toilet.

Signing off for the season with a goal in a crazy 5-5 draw at West Brom, Robin van Persie could put his feet up for a well-earned summer break after a season that had pushed his career onto another level.

Gareth Bale scooped the end of season PFA player of the year award, but his team had finished down in fifth place while his Welsh national side stood no realistic hope of qualifying for the 2014 World Cup in Brazil. The Netherlands, meanwhile, were seven points clear at the top of their group with just four games remaining. What would Bale have given to swap places?

After watching van Persie lead his club and country from

the front – he scored three goals in the qualifying games against Estonia and Romania – Netherlands manager Louis van Gaal named van Persie as his team's captain. For a man who once spent time in jail on remand to be given the captain's armband capped a remarkable turnaround not only in his career but in his life.

As he approached 30 years of age, van Persie was now a dependable goalscorer at the highest level and somebody younger players could look up to. A new era was set to dawn at Old Trafford with some of the elder statesmen of the club pondering their own retirements, and with Scholes calling it a day Ryan Giggs was the only remaining original 'Fergie Fledgling'. With a tiny wisp of grey hair already beginning to sneak its way into his carefully chiselled block of hair, younger players like 20-year-old Wilfried Zaha would be looking up to him for advice.

Capturing the Champions League trophy and winning some silverware as captain of the Netherlands were two things he could aspire to in the short term, but his growth as a leader would also prove important in the overall direction of his career. René Meulensteen, assistant to Ferguson at the time he retired, told Danish newspaper *Algemeen Dagblad* that he felt there was a coach hiding inside van Persie. He had worked hard on team-bonding exercises at Arsenal – allegedly hiring a karaoke machine and encouraging the squad to sing pop songs – and was somebody younger players felt they could go to.

Recuperation time during any future injury lay-offs could be put to good use by starting to earn coaching badges. Ryan Giggs was completing coaching badges while still playing and was immediately appointed player-coach when

David Moyes took over at Old Trafford, so his progress will be worth monitoring and emulating.

Building man-management skills is an important process in any profession. When his body no longer allows him to lead from the front on the pitch, van Persie must be ready to lead from the dugout.